THE CREATIVE GARDENER

STEPHANIE MAHON
Photography by
JOHN CAMPBELL

THE CREATIVE GARDENER

INSPIRING PEOPLE, REMARKABLE GARDENS

FRANCES LINCOLN

CONTENTS

PREVIOUS A pretty planted display in an old agricultural trough, typical of the thoughtful modern rustic aesthetic at Alison Jenkins's Damson Farm near Bath. **FACING** Farrah Storr's charming summerhouse and attached mini greenhouse in her Kent garden.

INTRODUCTION

I WAS FOURTEEN when I decided I wanted to be a writer. I imagined myself living a buzzy, busy, creative life somewhere cosmopolitan and achingly cool. My parents weren't convinced, having hoped I'd follow my mother into dentistry, but several summers scraping wax off dental instruments in her surgery cured me of that.

Having slacked through university, and taken a series of jobs from being a personal assistant to working in a Christmas theme park, I talked my way into my first proper role on a magazine and then to newspapers. The Irish economic boom of the late 1990s and early 2000s was well underway, with a burgeoning media scene, and it was a fun place to be young and forging a path. I was writing for a living, and that seemed miraculous. But something was missing, and it nagged at me.

I grew up on the edge of a market town, a commuter's drive from Dublin. My grandfather helped my parents buy our house on the understanding that he would be popping over every weekend to garden it like his own, and he dug up the front lawn to grow carrots and potatoes, and plant raspberry bushes and herbs. Once he died, however, with four kids, no time and little interest, my parents dismantled his greenhouse and grassed over the veg beds, and our short dalliance with gardening faded into childhood memory, with only some stubborn rhubarb left to show for it.

As a mardy teenager I would walk the hinterland of the town where urban sprawl meets fields of sheep and all the footpaths suddenly end. My favourite place to mitch off Mass on a Sunday morning was a little grove of hawthorn trees behind the church, hidden from passersby by enormous tangled sweeps of brambles. I'd sit in the rough grass and think what I imagined were incredibly deep thoughts, and find some brief peace. All that time spent propped against a tree trunk observing nature made it my default decompression mechanism.

So I knew enough about myself as I got older to seek out landscapes and countryside where I could, and even attempted to buy a couple of rundown old cottages in the middle of nowhere – but anything with standing walls and a roof was out of my price range. I abandoned the idea of creating my own place, and decided to go travelling to see if I could find the missing thing out in the world somewhere.

I ended up in a ramshackle old castle in Italy, helping my friend Clark run a cheap and cheerful, chip-in-with-the-washing-up sort of B&B, offering cultural happenings such as reading retreats, art exhibitions and classical music concerts. On a shoestring, we dreamed up wild themed events where we turned the barn into a pirate ship and scared people silly in the 'haunted' woods for Halloween. There was a lot of cleaning and cooking, but it was also like a dinner party every night with interesting people from all over the world eating under the Atlas cedar hung with twinkling tealights.

There was a bohemian romance to it all, from sleeping at the top of the fourteenth-century tower on hot summer nights to huddling in our one heated room during quiet, guest-lite winters. Every day was a step into the unknown. Would our guests turn up? If they did, would they stay once they learned they had to share a bathroom? Would any more of the roof fall down today? How late could we pay the rent this month? And just how do you cook stew for three hundred people?

PREVIOUS The swimming pond at Will Tomson's Berrywell in South Yorkshire. **FACING** The colourful entrance borders with towering aralias at Jimi Blake's Hunting Brook in Co. Wicklow, Ireland.

Clark was interested in gardening, and I was not. He was determined to make the acres around the crumbling castle beautiful, but the garden was a dumping ground of rubbish and old fridges, and so overgrown with cherry laurel that he was quite surprised, upon cutting it back, to discover an old fountain at the centre.

I helped out in the veg beds and the flower borders, but admit that it took a while for the horticultural bug to bite. The way Clark got me in the end was through making a database of plants – I am a sucker for a good list. The plant names were fun to learn, especially when set to music – try singing *Ceratostigma plumbaginoides* the tune of Barry Manilow's 'Copacabana' – or altered to be smutty enough to remember.

Somewhere along the way, through the hours and days of gardening – weeding the cobblestone paths, raking up millions of *Magnolia grandiflora* leaves, and all the standing and staring and talking about what we were creating – I felt a welcome shift. I had found the thing.

Even now, so many years later, having made other gardens, studied horticulture and become a garden writer and editor for a living, gardening is what sustains me. It heals, fuels and inspires me. When I lose perspective, it brings me back to myself, and through the terrible and the wonderful it is a true constant. Whatever happens in life, I know that the act of gardening is a gift that I can carry with me anywhere.

Through my work, I have been lucky enough to meet many people who feel the same unashamed devotion to the craft, and whose expression of it captivates me. What I have come to realize is that no one is born a creative gardener; it isn't a talent that appears fully formed. They are made slowly through exposure and repetition, and the learned skill of noticing small things. There are no prodigies here and no shortcuts. It's not something that can be copied and pasted, downloaded or delegated. Instead, it is built through time spent engaging with plants and soil and air, and everything in between. It's about the 'doing' rather than the end result.

So, this book is not about gardens as pristine finished objects, but the people who make them and what their practice of gardening and growing means to them. Across these pages are the stories of twenty-seven 'hortists' – my awkwardly coined term to encompass all the different types of horticultural artist and artist-gardener featured within.

Many of them arrived at gardening via circuitous routes, through art, food, writing, music, science, social care or even by chance. One thing they all share, however, is curiosity. They look, question and experiment. They learn by making enough mistakes that their experience fosters intuition. Trying, and probably messing up, over and over develops a way of thinking and being that is becoming increasingly scarce, but perhaps more and more necessary, in our time.

I was struck again and again in my interviews by how willing people were to flip their lives and jump into the unknown – ditching a great job to retrain or start over in a new industry, or remortgaging or ploughing a life's worth of savings into a new business. But many looked puzzled when I asked if they ever worried about their big gambles paying off.

To them, it seemed so obvious. Failure is part of life, and the threat of it should never stop you from reaching for something. This acceptance of uncertainty reflects something every gardener must learn. The weather will never do as you wish, plants will probably die and you will never have enough time. Learning to live with these disappointments is a lesson in resilience that can stand you in good stead outside the garden as well.

The majority of these gardeners started out with very little land or money, and almost all began without a plan. They show that constraints don't have to be the enemy – as most parents and creatives will tell you, boundaries can be a good thing. Every gardener works within limits, whether it's the size of their plot or budget, their soil or aspect, or having to also manage full-time jobs, young children, illness or grief.

None of them waited for the ideal conditions. Instead, they improvised and worked with what was already there. In the garden, perfection is not possible or even particularly desirable. A creative gardener doesn't impose their vision on a space and force it through. Instead, they learn when to intervene and when to step back. They give up the idea of

FACING Josh Sparkes brings in a box of produce at Birch Farm in Devon, with a little help from Twinkle the dog.

control to make way for a more fulfilling relationship with their plot. Because, as all gardeners know, gardens are never 'done'. They are constantly changing, through every day and season, and as our own lives change.

A common thread running through many of the conversations I had for this book was the garden as a sanctuary, a place that can absorb both joy and loss, offering safety, spiritual sustenance and continuity when other things fall apart. And when these spaces are shared, they become important gathering spaces of connection and community too.

For some, gardens are a canvas upon which they can paint with nature, a living art installation with the challenging, complicating factors of plants and time. For others, they offer raw materials or subjects and models. Gardens feed us with beauty and ideas as well as flowers and vegetables. They can even be epicentres of innovation where experimentation sparks a mini revolution in thinking and a movement for change.

For those for whom gardening is not their primary work – the writers, artists, designers, illustrators, performers and makers – the garden often provides mental clarity. With your hands in the soil, ideas are loosened and problems are put into perspective. As your body is engaged, the mind settles and connections can be made sideways rather than head-on. Inspiration, it turns out, doesn't only appear in fabled eureka-like moments of mania, but also through the quiet and often dull rhythms of weeding, watering, sowing or planting.

Something else I hope to illustrate is that no garden is made alone. Partners, parents, children, friends, mentors, colleagues, volunteers, collaborators and neighbours all appear throughout these chapters, alongside pets, wildlife and the weather. Gardens are collective works and I was determined, when I came to write about these creative gardeners, to reflect their full selves and lives as parents of young kids or as jobbing gardeners chasing a dream. And I wanted to openly acknowledge those, rarely named, who are the real backbone of so many gardens, and the support system without whom nothing would succeed.

Just as all life is here, so these growing spaces span the gamut from country gardens that are tended daily to scrappy allotments where someone might grab an hour on the weekend. The gardeners in this book are not united by style or status, but by values. They care about how things are made, not just how they look, and they accept responsibility for the choices they make and the spaces they shape. Ethics are just as important, if not more so, than aesthetics.

You won't find a step-by-step guide in these pages about how to unleash your inner creative gardener, or a manual with practical tips. It's more of a philosophy or perhaps even a manifesto of why and how gardening matters – not as decoration or diversion, but as a vital creative practice.

If you'd like to be more of a creative gardener, then the key lessons I have gleaned from my time with these generous and talented people are these: be curious, be patient, be bold ... and just care. For to garden creatively is to project hope – a special kind of hope that is grounded in action. And that is something we are sure to need more of, now and in the future.

FACING TOP A long lean-to greenhouse and the old Victorian well in the Kitchen Garden at Knepp in West Sussex, where Charlie Harpur leads the team. **FACING BOTTOM** A 'niffed' rose, with its bare winter stems sculpted into an incredible wave shape by Jenny Barnes.

ALISON JENKINS

A FEW MILES outside the city of Bath, tucked into the lee of a lush green valley, lies Damson Farm, the home and garden of Alison Jenkins. Her path to this special place has meandered from the art world to garden design, and now her self-made role as a sort of knowledge curator and community facilitator.

'I have been developing the garden as a gathering place to have conversations and figure out how we need to garden differently,' she says. 'To question the ways that we've been doing things, and explore ideas.' She leads workshops herself, using the garden as a teaching aid, and also hosts specialists in their fields to deliver courses on everything from permaculture and cut-flower growing to composting and fibre making (creating twine and other fibres from plants).

'I'm quite interested in our ancestors' relationship with plants, and keeping that knowledge going. How do you make string from nettles or dandelions? Which plants can you use for dyeing? I want to hang on to and celebrate all of those skills we used to have.' Even as a child, she was drawn to plants and gardens. 'When I was small we had a really magical garden in North Wales, with a sunken rose garden, a big oak tree with a tyre swing, and a little summer house. Then we moved to a town, Market Drayton in Shropshire, when I was eleven, and I remember going into our new garden and thinking, "Oh, this doesn't feel right." I found a seedling of a beech tree and planted it right in the middle – I had this feeling that it needed to be filled with more plants and trees.'

It never occurred to her that she could make gardens into a career – 'It just wasn't ever presented as an option' – so she ended up going into the art world. 'I'm not sure I had the confidence to be an artist, but I was drawn to working in galleries. It was something about the idea of creating spaces.'

Alison did a multidisciplinary arts degree, and volunteered at the Bath Festival, which led to her first job as a gallery assistant, and then another at a gallery on the Portobello Road in London. She progressed to a masters in art history and freelancing as an exhibition organizer, with stints at the Photographer's Gallery and the Serpentine Gallery. From the outside, it looked like an incredible, gold-dust career in an exciting creative industry. 'But I was spending my weekends writing essays and looking out the window, thinking that, actually, I want to be outside. Organizing exhibitions was a lot of logistics, sitting in front of the computer. I started thinking about moving in a different direction.'

Always upskilling, she studied horticulture at night and jumped into working as a freelance maintenance gardener. Her clients asked her to do design work too, so she trained at the English Gardening School and set up as a designer. 'I really enjoyed creating little sanctuaries for people for when they came home from work in the city. It felt like those were quite essential spaces where people could be among plants. And that's always the thing I enjoyed most about the design side: creating spaces that feel nourishing and safe in the midst of a harsh world.'

Alison moved to Bath in 2002 and continued to design, but over time the same issues that had turned her off gallery work began to creep in. 'I was doing a lot of admin. There are so many layers to getting gardens built in terms of engineering, drainage, health and safety, and all the legislation. I was thinking, this doesn't feel like why I got into gardening in the first place. I wanted to find a way back to the practice of gardening, and figure out how to be a better gardener, or how to evolve a garden practice, given that we're in an era of environmental crisis.'

Damson Farm was to become the answer, with its stone-built, wisteria-draped Victorian cottage and over half a hectare (2 acres) of land. Alison used to look after a garden further up the valley and always had her eye on the property, so when it did eventually come up for sale, it didn't matter that the house was quite run down. 'I fell in love with the site – we hardly even looked at the house. I went straight out to the garden, which was just a sloping field. I don't think anybody had gardened here for a very long time.'

Her new hillside was steep and east facing, but blessed with a deep layer of rich topsoil over clay. Alison was beyond busy at this point, however, with a two year old and a design practice to run, so she didn't launch into a grand scheme for the plot straight away, instead letting it evolve over many years.

The first layer of the garden you experience, draped like a floral shawl around the house, is a cultivated ornamental space. Sitting at the long table in the airy, double-height kitchen – perfect for workshop groups to gather and eat – glazed doors to the north and south give on to wonderful views.

To the north is an expansive scene out to a stone terrace with steps up to the meadow and countryside beyond. To the south, there's a more interior view to an intimate courtyard garden. Low retaining walls clad in rusted mild steel help to manage the changes in level and create a central flat area, where a charming spring-fed rill runs from one trough to another, and the lime-yellow flowers of *Alchemilla mollis* froth in abundance. Large characterful blobs of clipped evergreen *Phillyrea latifolia* hold the space, giving blocks of tall perennials including *Eupatorium* 'Riesenschirm' and *Veronicastrum virginicum* 'Album' the freedom to let it all hang out.

ABOVE Alison's kitchen, where she hosts workshop groups, looks out on to a courtyard with domes of clipped evergreen *Phillyrea latifolia*. **FACING TOP** The courtyard features a rill and perennials such as lady's mantle and sanguisorba. Beyond, a planted slope rises up to the rest of the garden. **FACING BOTTOM** At the top of the slope, the deck outside Alison's mezzanine level office features old steel tubs and troughs of interesting edibles and companion flowers. **OVERLEAF** Mown paths through the meadow lead to the kitchen garden, which is framed with rust-coloured estate fencing and small beds of flowers.

Tucked in the corner, sheltered by the walls of the house and a small lean-to greenhouse, is a small gravel garden where bronze spires of *Digitalis ferruginea* happily seed themselves around, and a wall-trained apricot – 'one of the first things I planted' – decides each year whether it will provide a bumper crop of delicious fruit, or none.

At the back of the courtyard, the ground rises steeply up a slope planted with stalwarts such as the ornamental grass *Calamagrostis brachytricha* and the well-behaved *Acanthus* 'Rue Ledan'. Climb the steps to the top and at the back of the house you'll find Alison's unusual mezzanine-level office, with a deck outside that features old salvaged steel bathtubs and metal agricultural troughs planted with pretty displays of salads and unusual edibles like lablab.

From here, the land flows into a shaggy orchard, which started out as 'the standard lawn for paddling pools and bouncy castles for birthday parties'. Once the need for such things diminished, the rectangle of mown grass was reduced to a path, and twelve years on – with a little help from yellow rattle to keep the grass down – it is a meadow woven through with wild flowers including orchids, ragged robin, wild carrot and angelica. 'It's quite interesting to see what's coming in now of its own accord. It almost feels like it's letting the land breathe.'

A ribbon of fruit trees runs through, heavy with apples and plums. Alison cuts the long grass down in stages in mid- to late summer, leaving small haystacks to cure here and there 'to leave refuge for all the crickets and little frogs'. It makes for an idyllic pastoral scene. After leaving the stacks to sit for a couple of months, she uses the hay to make compost cakes – free-standing, artful cylinders of cut-down vegetation, upon which she grows mounds of happy squash plants, so they don't take up space in the edible garden next door.

This productive space, the first area Alison created, is where she spends most of her gardening time. She got a digger in to level it off and built a series of small, slightly raised beds – 'easier to manage and maintain in small chunks' – using the classic no-dig method of cardboard and compost. Paths of pebbly gravel run through and host swathes of self-seeders and joyful spreaders like mint and alpine strawberries, which she is happy to leave.

FACING TOP The raised beds feature a mix of traditional vegetables and fruit with lesser-known varieties and ornamental grasses and flowers. **FACING BOTTOM LEFT** Alison makes all of her own amazing plant supports, from arches to obelisks, from coppiced hazel and willow. **FACING BOTTOM RIGHT** Reusing items and giving them new life is part of her philosophy, such as using this old sewing machine base as a pot display table. **ABOVE** Alison creates compost cakes from the cut-down meadow hay and then grows squash and pumpkins in them.

'That's always the thing I enjoyed most about the design side: creating spaces that feel nourishing and safe in the midst of a harsh world.'

FACING Alison harvests plants for salads, cut flowers, seeds and fibres throughout the season. **ABOVE** The hill above the house features many fruit trees in long grass, with islands of more curated planting, and offers wonderful views across the valley.

Alison does grow in rows, with neat, netted sections of purple sprouting broccoli and cavalo nero, but this is beautifully counteracted by jumbled flowery fringes of nicotiana, cosmos, poppies and zinnias, and herbs including borage, oregano and Korean mint. There are rainbow chard and nasturtiums, tree spinach and sunflowers, roses and raspberries.

She points out an unusual radish grown for its seed pods and a nasturtium relative grown for its tubers, as well as more typical peas, beans and asparagus. Blackberries and wineberries drape over the drystone wall at the perimeter, which features cubbyholes known as bee boles: alcoves where skeps were once placed to collect honey from wild swarms.

Its function may be to feed, but the edible garden undeniably looks smart, with rust-coloured estate fencing and handmade hazel supports that range in ambition and design from a tunnel arch to A-frames and teepees, with exquisite artistic detailing. 'I think beauty is a really important factor,' says Alison. 'I'm interested in permaculture, but it exists in quite a different world than garden design. Wouldn't it be great if there could be more crossover? Because as human beings we respond to beauty, and places that make us feel good.'

Practicality is still important, and Alison has a shed and a glasshouse where she grows aubergines, Padron peppers (an old heritage cultivar) and tomatoes, including her new favourite, 'Brad's Atomic Grape', whose seeds always come true. 'The tomatoes I've been saving seed from, for about three years now, do seem stronger and more resilient, because they're adapting each time to the local conditions.'

She also grows cucamelons to pickle – 'I like something that you can put on the shelf' – but the harvests she enjoys most are salads full of colour and flavour, foraged from the garden for workshop groups to devour. 'I love putting together a salad with loads of different types of leaves, herbs and edible flowers. With thirty different things you know that, nutritionally, it's going to be really good.'

Growing food can be time and resource heavy, but Alison tries to be as sustainable as possible, using a rainwater harvesting tank to irrigate young plants and mulching in various ways to keep moisture in the soil. 'I try not to grow things that need too much cosseting, but I do use sheep's wool around my dahlias. I have given up trying to grow carrots, and the pigeons stripped all the peas this year. Sometimes you just have to be philosophical and say, okay, that's just what happened this year.'

We like to feel that we're in control, she muses, but gardening teaches you that we are not. 'I think that's the difference between being a visual artist, in painting or sculpture, where you make something in the studio and that's it; that's your creation. Whereas when you're working in the garden, it's not just you. You're working with natural elements, and plants that might have their own ideas about things. The weather is increasingly unpredictable. There are lots of unknown quantities, and you have to put your ego to one side and recognize that you're working in partnership.'

We trek up the meadow slopes to the highest reaches of the garden, where a small flock of sheep graze and tucked in behind a small pond and overhanging willow tree lies a fire pit with a circle of stone seats. It's a good spot for groups to hang out, enjoy some elemental vibes and take in the views across the valley.

Is it challenging, I wonder, to open up your home and garden to relative strangers? 'It pushes me to keep learning and doing new things,' Alison replies. 'And it's a huge privilege having this space. So to be able to share it, for other people to get something from it, makes sense. It would feel too much of an indulgence just to be doing it for my own sake.'

FACING Shasta daisies ebulliently spreading to fill the space around Alison's hard-working greenhouse, where she propagates plants, sows seeds and grows more tender vegetables such as tomatoes and aubergines.

NIGEL SLATER

'THERE'S NEVER BEEN a time when a garden wasn't a priority in my life,' says Nigel Slater. The much-loved cook, writer and broadcaster, best known for his flavourful recipes for seasonal comfort dishes, is at pains to paint himself as just an amateur, but has to admit that he has been gardening since he was a young boy.

After much pestering, his father gave him a patch of soil in their Wolverhampton plot. 'It turned out it was the most difficult bit of the garden, the one that he didn't really want – but everything I planted grew. I went through the seed catalogues, chose my plants, bought them with my pocket money and put them in, and they worked. There's something about being eleven years old and a seed you've sown actually growing that is so exciting.'

Nigel spent time in the greenhouses at his country school as a teenager, and enjoyed picking herbs in the hotel garden of his first job as a chef, but it was only once he moved to London in his early twenties that his childhood passion began to reassert itself.

He lived vicariously through other people's gardens at first, helping out a landlady who always forgot to water her sweet peas and mow her lawn. He recalls, too, stuffing the window boxes of an attic room with courgette and tomato plants, and the communal garden of his first flat, where 'you had to have a meeting before you could do anything'.

His present garden, behind his immaculately considered home in Highbury, north London, is small but perfectly formed, and has been through several stages since he first moved in twenty-five years ago. 'At first, it was a blank canvas, which was lovely because it's a bit like having that first blank page in your notebook when you're starting a book,' he says. 'Anything is possible.'

He was keen to remove the bamboo and some rather municipal-looking grey panelling, but kept a large robinia tree and set his sights on growing food. Thanks to his weekly column in the *Observer*, which Monty Don also wrote for at the time, the man himself came over and drew up a basic plan to get him started.

'What he got me to understand was that although it is one garden, it has different spaces: there's a dark side of the garden and a bright side, a damp side and a dry side. He helped me understand what I could grow best in those different microclimates, and I stuck to his words like glue.'

Soon Nigel had beds of brassicas and herbs, roots and salad, and a bevy of beautiful fruit and nut trees, including damson, plum, quince, greengage, apple, medlar, mulberry and cobnut. This incarnation of the garden was incredibly pleasurable and rewarding but hard work, and the bounty was not to last. 'It took a lot of time to tend, and the limitations of space began to hit home. I could plant carrots, but it wasn't going to keep me in carrots for the year.'

The main issue, however, was the havoc caused by unwanted visitors to the garden. 'I lost my battle with the foxes from next door,' Nigel explains. 'They wrecked everything. I'd get up in the morning and look out the window and there would be devastation: my wigwams with sweet peas, nasturtiums and little baby pumpkins all smashed to pieces where the cubs had been playing and fighting.'

The fruit trees also proved a challenge. 'I hadn't thought about the fact that the garden is only 35 metres (115 feet) long, so they all grew together, which didn't do them much good. It also meant the many squirrels could bounce from one tree to another, like parkour, eating everything along their way.'

Although he still grows herbs and tomatoes in pots now – 'I never want to not grow some food' – Nigel decided to drastically change the garden so it was more creature-proof. He took out the veg beds and some of the fruit trees, and transformed it into an ornamental garden. This time, he got advice from another *Observer* columnist, the designer Dan Pearson, who introduced him to woodland treasures like epimedium and brunnera for the shady side of the garden.

Nigel has adapted and tweaked the layout and planting further himself since then, but mulls over ideas a lot before changing anything, such as whether to swap the gravel paths for reclaimed stone. One decision he has never regretted, however, was splitting the long, thin garden up into three 'rooms' with yew hedging. Put in as small whips, these evergreen fortresses are now so enormous that Nigel's regular gardening help, Katie, isn't sure she can clip them anymore.

The first, largest room you encounter as you step out from the house has the character of an English country garden, but modernized and in miniature, with restrained, tasteful echoes of the Arts & Crafts abundance of Sissinghurst, Hidcote and Great Dixter.

'I wanted little bits of gardens I had seen and knew – it wasn't a total reinvention. I tend to take something that is quite familiar, friendly and loved, like a style of garden or a recipe, and then put my own imprint on it. It's not reinventing the wheel; it's taking something traditional or that's been done before and refreshing it, putting my own signature on it.'

The steps down to the stone terrace are populated with clipped evergreen balls in terracotta pots, and overhung with wisteria – one of several Nigel grows, which climb and sprawl, reaching their tendrils up into hedges and the large fig tree in the corner. Underneath there's a generous bench and low table stacked with pots of herbs, so he can pop out easily from his test kitchen to grab thyme, rosemary or tarragon for whatever dish he is trying out that day.

Passing between the symmetrical sentinels of two tall beech topiaries, the path is lined with terracotta pots of successional blooms, from tulips in spring and foxgloves in early summer to dahlias as the garden slides into autumn. There are yew domes and box balls for formal structure, but also climbers such as honeysuckle and jasmine that ramble with louche confidence along the edges of the scene. 'Things that you're never totally in control of, so they make the garden feel a bit wild and romantic,' says Nigel.

A large zinc-topped oak table holds the centre of the space, with beds of peachy-hued roses and pastel perennials on either side. The sunlight dappling through the trees illuminates Nigel's tabletop pots, which he plants up with bulbs, such as daffodils and crocus, for spring and with pelargoniums for summer. He sometimes likes to write here when it's warm, under the shade of the crooked-limbed robinia, surrounded by fragrant flowers.

He recently cut back a lot of dense growth at the boundaries, opening the garden up to the light, and enabling him to plant more of his favourites, especially roses. 'I'm not impulsive – I think about things for a long time – but I surprise myself at my ruthlessness. With an urban garden such as this, every inch is precious. I'd love more space, but I know within a year I'd fill it.'

A black metal gate in the hedge opens on to the second, shadier room – a smaller space with a large old copper pot, set on a plinth covered in moss, as a focal point. Around this Nigel grows shade-loving shrubs such as acer, azalea, edgeworthia and daphne. Beneath their limbs, the ground layer includes pittosporum balls, and springtime treats in shades of white, yellow and pink, including cyclamen, snowdrops, hepaticas, primroses and wood anemones, followed by columbine and bleeding heart. In June, jaw-dropping dogwood *Cornus* 'Gloria Birkett', with pink-tinged white bracts, puts on a show. 'It's a sort of imaginary woodland,' says Nigel. 'More Japanese than British, with layers of green and a few flowers.'

The third room is a tiny space, in full shade, where ferns and sweet woodruff spread themselves around. Pride of place is taken by an old broken terracotta pot that Nigel lovingly reconstructed with wire, in what must be a nod to the two Japanese concepts of *wabi-sabi* and *kintsugi*. Japan's customs,

PREVIOUS In summer, Nigel's garden features abundant foxgloves in pastel shades of pink, yellow, apricot and white, alongside roses and clipped box and beech shapes. **FACING** Through the gate into the second small room of the garden, Nigel has placed a patinated copper pot on a plinth covered in moss, under a blooming dogwood tree.

'It's not reinventing the wheel; it's taking something traditional or that's been done before and refreshing it, putting my own signature on it.'

FACING TOP The secret courtyard outside Nigel's basement kitchen is painted in a coral shade and features a large tree fern. **FACING BOTTOM** Nigel's collection of ferns bring a fresh green feel here, where Nigel does all his potting up. **TOP LEFT** The zinc-topped oak table in the centre of the main garden is sheltered by a crooked-limbed robinia tree. Nigel often writes here and likes to display pelargoniums in pots on the top. **TOP RIGHT** The doors of his test kitchen open straight on to the garden, with clipped evergreens in pots lining the steps and a halo of wisteria over the threshold.

philosophy, food and gardens are an endless inspiration to him and he travels there almost every year in spring.

Though this is the limit of the main garden, Nigel has one more surprise. Back by the house, down a flight of steps to the basement level, lies a secret courtyard with its own microclimate. Nigel has painted the walls of the house here a plaster-like apricot-orange, inspired by designer Arne Maynard's Welsh home, Allt y Bela. They give the perfect backdrop to the vibrant green ferns and moss that live here in pots under a canopy of scented jasmine. A tree fern basks on one wall, happy in the cosy atmosphere created by the outlet vent of the Aga. 'I've never wrapped it up in winter or done any of the things you're supposed to, and it keeps on growing.'

It's clear from the way Nigel speaks about his sanctuary, telling the story of each plant, how deeply he feels about this garden and how integral it is to his work, even if he's not growing much food any longer. He first realized the essential connection many years ago, while working at a country house in the Lake District. As he made scones, a chef told him to look out the window at the blazing drifts of daffodils running down to the water. 'He told me to put that picture into my food – it's like stirring the love in. If you look at something beautiful when you're cooking, spiritually, it's another seasoning, like a herb or spice.'

As well as providing beauty to imbue in his recipes, the garden is important as a release valve and creative escape. 'If I've written something a bit rubbish, stepping away from my desk and into the garden helps my brain clear. I'll spend twenty minutes out there and suddenly I see things differently and everything I'm doing falls into place. The confusion has gone, and I can start again or untangle that sentence. Simply going out into the garden recharges me – it's as if I've plugged into the mains.'

This energizing effect may be why he doesn't consider gardening all that relaxing. 'It's probably because I don't feel like I have enough time, just a snatched hour here or there, and there are always things that must be done. I've never walked out into the garden and thought it was wonderful, done, finished, sorted.' He sighs, not unhappily, and details the bulbs he has to sort for planting and the window boxes he needs to change over. 'Sometimes I go out there to potter and end up losing four or five hours. There is always something to do.'

ABOVE Nigel has a penchant for classic English garden flowers such as pinks. **FACING TOP** A stylish oak bench offers a place to sit beside a homemade table that is home to Nigel's culinary herbs. **FACING BOTTOM** At the very end of the garden, in the shadiest spot, is a small alcove with a much-loved broken pot which Nigel has mended with wire and care.

SARAH PRICE

SARAH PRICE has just been painting giant canvases. These are not artworks per se, but backdrops for a temporary garden installation she's creating on a shoestring. With anyone else, you might have reservations about how successful the result will be, but with Sarah it's always going to be good.

This is the designer who recycles waste into exquisite water bowls; she could probably make a pile of wellies look elegantly breathtaking. With an instinctive feel for natural beauty, she's the kind of once in a generation talent that leaves the rest of us slightly awestruck, wondering – how does she do it?

We're sitting in the newly refurbished glasshouse of her garden at the foothills of the Black Mountains in South Wales. 'My garden is my sketchbook, and it feeds me creatively,' she says. This was once her grandparents' home, so she has known it her entire life, spending holidays here as a child. 'Growing up, this garden was a place I could run around freely. I was an observant child, and I'd always be looking intently at nature. It felt very normal – I didn't realize it was particularly unusual. It was just something I loved and part of life.'

Another influence was her father's allotment. 'We would go there on Saturday mornings and it was a way I could get him alone – you don't get much one-on-one time in a house of five children.' They would also take long walks together to explore 'any wild place that my father would find on a map'.

While quite young, it became apparent that Sarah had artistic talent. 'Drawing was something that was mine, that people outside my family picked up on early. I am dyslexic, but my drawings were singled out in school, and I needed that acknowledgement; it meant a lot for my self-esteem.'

This recognition led to an obsession with art, and so it was not a surprise when she decided to study fine art at university. This was in that heady period of the early 2000s, still in thrall to the Young British Artists, when painting and crafts had been declared officially 'dead', so she embraced conceptual film and photographic possibilities, and dabbled in light installations, architecture and camera obscuras.

Sarah came top of her class, but noticed she had slipped into art-scene pretension when her parents couldn't understand her dissertation. 'I'd become disconnected from the real world.' She returned to Wales and spent time in the garden. 'After being in an urban environment, you realize how much the landscape means to you and how you get a level of deep calm when you're gardening. My grandmother had died, so I was trying desperately to keep this special space cared for, and my father was quite ill, so it was a lovely thing to do together.'

Sarah could see the alchemy her grandmother had created here. All the plants she had put in many years before were taking on their mature forms; the fruit cages were being taken over by poppies and cosmos. 'I felt so moved by these spaces and by nature in a way that I wasn't in a white cube of a gallery.'

This understanding led her to apply for an apprenticeship at Hampton Court Palace, but they were so impressed by her plant knowledge at interview that they offered her a job instead. 'I was mowing diamonds in the lawn and doing bedding plants, but it was relaxing in a strange way, and fun.' Garden design seemed like an obvious onward path, so she did a part-time course and began to build a portfolio, which led to freelance work, winning several competitions and doing two Chelsea Flower Show gardens for QVC in 2007 and 2008. People started to pay attention.

A magazine profile was picked up by a team of landscape architects putting in a bid for the 2012 Olympic Park in London,

and they invited her to join planting gurus James Hitchmough and Nigel Dunnett, who were already in on the pitch. She never expected to be included if they won, but once they did, she quickly tweaked that to be part of this enormous opportunity, she needed to give it everything. 'I would work through the night to send my ideas to the lead designer in America. My role became important as a kind of visualizer. It was all about trying to marry the British and American approaches, which were very different.'

It was an incredibly busy and productive time, and the innovative plantings across the park propelled them all into the international limelight. 'But then I had my first child, so my working capacity for the next decade was limited, which, honestly, was quite hard,' she says. 'I turned so many things down, and did gardens while literally carrying a newborn around in a sling.' She focused on family; did some writing at night 'with brain fog'; and took on the projects she could, including the Whitworth Gallery in Manchester, an installation for fashion brand Hermes and a garden for cancer charity Maggie's Centre in Southampton.

More recently, Sarah has created designs for The Exchange, a community arts centre in Erith, south-east London, and for the revival of Benton End, the former home and garden of artist-plantsman Cedric Morris, in Suffolk. 'I'm lucky to have had my career established before I had children, because you could easily lose confidence. I feel incredibly fortunate that I've been able to pick things back up.'

Many designers say show gardens do nothing for your career, but Sarah says all her work has come from them. Her 2023 Chelsea garden was widely declared the GOAT of show gardens – the greatest of all time. It was the ultimate combination of things she'd tried out before, from reclaimed materials and rammed earth walls to a modern Mediterranean plant palette, including the dusky hues of the Morris-bred Benton irises.

She freely admits she could do nothing without collaborators, whether they be the landscaping team from Crocus who do her show gardens or those skilled gardeners who look after her clients' designs once they are planted. 'Creating any garden is a huge collaboration of many talented people. The gardeners are the artists. You need someone who can read nature, who has the confidence to look at a plant and see what could be cut down now and what can be left. You're asking for a sensitive eye, a responsive person who is intelligent and artful. It's a highly skilled job that requires years of experience, because there isn't a specific rule book.'

And she wouldn't have her own garden, she says, without the talented help of her regular crew of Keri Schofield, Jacky Mills and Ian Mannall. 'They have all brought something different to the garden and do it in such a beautiful way. It's wonderful when you don't need to hover over people; they just get it.'

They also operate as sounding boards for her. 'I'll say, "Am I crazy thinking we should replant this area in recycled sand?" And everyone says, we should totally do that. When people are completely behind what you're doing, you do it; you're not constantly second guessing yourself.'

When she moved back to Wales from London in 2013, the walled garden was partly cultivated, with a productive area and patch of lawn. 'There were huge beds of ground elder under mature shrubs, and the secret garden was completely wild with brambles and laurel.'

Sarah has developed it slowly over the years, as and when she's had time and plants. 'I gardened it quite loosely when I first came, with dahlias and annuals, just chucking things in.' A few years on, though, having become convinced that its upkeep was more than she could manage, that experimental notion of the recycled sand started to look good.

Sarah and the team cleared and topped off the central section with recycled sand from a local quarry to a depth of 35 centimetres (14 inches), replanting with drought-resilient lovelies including euphorbias, eremurus, scabious and salvias. Low-input, lower maintenance and a boon for biodiversity, it worked so well that they have since repeated the idea across the walled garden. In another substrates experiment, they created rubble beds in the remains of the old cold frames

PREVIOUS The walled garden features a naturalistic mix of planting and focal points including a propped-up dead lilac tree, which brings character and offers a habitat for wildlife. **FACING TOP** Sarah brought in recycled sand to grow an exciting mix of plants including white umbel *Ligusticum lucidum*, various acid-yellow euphorbia and apricot spires of eremurus. **FACING BOTTOM** At the entrance to the walled garden, a small seating area is edged with homemade hazel hurdles and a selection of pretty pots.

'Creating any garden is a huge collaboration of many talented people. The gardeners are the artists.'

FACING TOP & BOTTOM The old greenhouse had a charming rustic quality before it was recently refurbished. Sarah uses it to grow tomatoes and grapes, dry onions and start off plants undercover. **TOP LEFT** In the wild garden, a small area loosely paved with stones dug up on site features a handmade bench and willow-woven edged beds under mature trees. **TOP RIGHT** Sarah has artfully trained several hornbeams and the unexpected native woody plants that arrived on site, such as hawthorns, into Japanese-style cloud shapes in the long grass.

along the front of the greenhouse, where succulents such as aeoniums now lend an otherworldly air.

At the edge of the sand beds stands a lean, and leaning, dead tree propped up on supports, working a double shift as both a sculptural element and standing deadwood for wildlife. Opposite lie a row of neat beds filled with rhubarb, gooseberries, runner beans, tomatoes, courgettes and purple sprouting broccoli. This is the domain of Sarah's husband, the author Jack Thurston, who practises no-dig growing and 'is a very good cook'.

The secret garden is reached via a small low tunnel which runs under the road. Ducking down to hobble, hunched, along the cobbled path in the dark, you soon forget the sun-soaked space you've left behind and emerge out the other end, in a rush of cool air, to a whole other scene of long grass and wild flowers under a canopy of tall trees and the sound of a gushing stream.

The deep, dense vegetation is cut through with skinny winding paths and dotted with characterful volunteer hawthorn bushes and oak saplings, which Sarah has been gently shaping in the *niwaki* style – a Japanese cloud pruning technique – but looser. They bring a welcome sense of structure and an indication of intention to this wonderfully woolly, sloping space, as do several humped dwarf fruit trees with arching branches that hang heavy with pears and apples.

The pond further along was dug out by hand. It can be traversed, with an inner trill of fear, via a slim timber slab of a bridge carved with markings made by local landscape artist Mick Petts. From the centre, surrounded all around by the reflected sky, you have the perfect view out across the garden to the Blorenge mountain in the distance.

We shuffle back through the tunnel and out of the walled garden, down steps under the trees, following the course of the stream. The path leads out to the lawn in front of the house, sections of which she leaves to grow long in summer with paths mown through. In the tangled woodland meadow beyond there is a sweet little shack they call the clover house, as well as the beginnings of a crafted dead hedge.

Sarah has plans for developing this area of the garden in the future, but has to take slow steps as the property – a large Victorian rectory – is now split into several homes. 'Technically it's not my garden; I share it with other people. But it's interesting seeing how spaces are used by people of different ages in a communal garden. It gives you a more sensitive outlook for when you're working with clients.'

The lucky few who do commission her benefit from this thoughtful approach. On starting a new project, she will go to the site and see 'what beauty can be drawn out'. Then she collages and draws quite a 'primitive' visual to set the mood, theme and tone. If she has time, she likes to create models by hand to explore the space.

But it's once the build begins that it gets really exciting for her. 'I love the moment when you're on site, taking things down and putting things in, and you're seeing space and void and colour, and shifting shadows and light. Often you've got to be like a conductor, controlling all these moving parts, and syncing it up.'

Sarah points out the blue-grey flower of a hibiscus her grandmother planted years ago. 'Just seeing these different colours or the way the petals fold can trigger ideas. To be constantly observing is a big inspiration. I walk around the garden every day and get an immense peace and creative spark back from it. There's so much to discover,' she says, with an enigmatic smile. 'There's just not enough time, is there?'

FACING The pond in the wild garden is crossed via a handcrafted timber bridge, and offers a scenic panorama of the house and the mountains beyond.

PROSPECT COTTAGE

JONNY BRUCE

'HORTICULTURE IS A pretty staid, conservative field,' says Jonny Bruce. The nurseryman is riffing on Prospect Cottage in Dungeness – former home of the late artist-director and gay rights activist Derek Jarman – where he has long been custodian of its landmark garden. 'If you look at what Derek did here, it's remarkable that he achieved something radically new within eight years. It's such a short amount of time to make a garden, and do something that changed the way we look at gardens.'

The garden in the shingle around the black-boarded house – now a site of pilgrimage for Jarman devotees – famously does not have a boundary. In 1986, when Jarman bought the plot on a flat, stark Kent beach with a view of the nearby power station, this was a very different approach to garden making. 'It made people question, what is a garden, or what does something need to be to become a garden?'

These sorts of interrogations are the reason that Jonny was first – and is still – captivated by this place. For him, what is intriguing is the art and meaning of gardens. Coming from an artistic family and having little passion for anything else, a creative life seemed the obvious choice, but it took a while to realize that something as seemingly stuffy and practical as gardening could offer everything he wanted.

He studied art history at Girton College, Cambridge, where, filled with a youthful verve to be self-sufficient and live more sustainably, he petitioned to start a student allotment. 'We grew moth-eaten cabbages for the student canteen, which was fun. But I loved the garden-making aspect of it. I wanted to provide a space that was an antidote to the intensity of people's coursework. I bought some old pub tables, hosted events, and realized that my motivation wasn't actually growing food. I wanted creative expression, and the garden facilitated that.'

The allotment was a welcome sanctuary as Jonny became increasingly disillusioned with his choice of course and the career path it would inevitably lead to. 'Suddenly I was in the mix with incredibly serious students who had five-year plans about which auction house they were going to intern at. They were very professionally minded, and I wasn't on the same wavelength at all. I saw myself on a conveyor belt into a contemporary art world job, and panicked. In my second year, I failed to submit a single essay on time, because I was so worried about it.'

Working on farms and gardens abroad in the holidays was a cheap and easy way to travel, and that summer Jonny went to Florence, spending time with Nick Dakin-Elliot, head gardener at Villa La Pietra. 'One day, I told him I was thinking of dropping out of Cambridge. "Why don't you be a gardener?" he said. "You obviously love plants." I went quiet, and sat with that for a little bit. In Britain, at that time, politicians were comparing gardening to litter picking, and referring to it as a job you should consider if you'd failed your GCSEs. But in Florence, gardens are fused with this idea of art history. In the Renaissance, horticulture was seen as a higher form of artistic expression than even painting or sculpture.'

While in Italy, Jonny was also reading *Modern Nature*, Derek Jarman's book about making the garden at Prospect Cottage after discovering he was HIV positive. 'That had a massive impact on me. It was something that felt very profound, like it had been written for me. I'd had a slightly prejudiced idea about what a garden was – window dressing for wealthy people's houses, rather than something with

ABOVE Prospect Cottage is situated in the driest place in Britain and within view of the nearby power station. **FACING TOP** The garden famously has no boundaries and is open to the surrounding beach. **FACING BOTTOM** The native sea kale that grows on the beach survives and thrives in the garden alongside foxgloves and red hot pokers.

conceptual depth. In reading *Modern Nature*, I realized that they could be so much more.' Jonny decided there and then that he was going to be a gardener, and all the anxiety about his course and future melted away.

He even decided to do his dissertation on the garden at Prospect Cottage. 'I felt that much more onus should be put on Derek as a gardener. At that time, he was often presented as a filmmaker and painter who sometimes gardened as a bit of a hobby, whereas my investigation into the garden was that this was actually his most significant artwork.'

Jarman was not a trained horticulturist and taught himself mostly out of books. 'He had a vision of a romantic, traditional, English cottage garden with roses and hollyhocks, but quickly realized that the environment here wasn't going to allow him to grow that type of garden.'

Often described as bleak, forbidding or desolate, Dungeness is classified as Britain's only desert. It is buffeted by bracing salty winds off the North Sea. There is little rainfall and next to no soil. It would be hard to find a more hostile place to grow. Changing course, Jarman went on instinct and integrated the wild plants of the ness, from dog roses to sea kale, alongside garden plants like poppies. He used beachcombed driftwood to mark where he had planted them, and created sculptures out of the flotsam that washed up on the shingle. It was an original and, before long, iconic take on a garden.

Jarman died in 1994, so Jonny never met him, but did get to know his long-time companion, Keith Collins, while researching his thesis. Jonny volunteered to help Keith in the garden, sometimes staying at the house and eventually having his own set of keys. 'It was such a special thing to get to know the garden in an intimate way, and learn how to garden it with Keith.'

When Collins became ill in 2018, he asked Jonny to look after Prospect in his stead. Since his death, Jonny has continued to look after the garden, and supported the 2020 fundraising campaign to save the cottage for the nation. It's now managed by the arts organization Creative Folkestone and hosts artist-in-residency programmes and public visit days.

The garden, although not large, is a big responsibility. Some people feel that it and the cottage interior should be perfectly preserved as they were, while others would prefer to transform the garden utterly to make a bold statement. But Jonny is

‘If you look at what Derek did here, it’s remarkable that he achieved something radically new within eight years.’

FACING The poem ‘The Sunne Rising’ by John Donne covers one wall of the famous black-stained house. **TOP LEFT** Plants in the garden such as gorse are echoed in the landscape of Dungeness. **TOP RIGHT** Drought-tolerant Mediterranean plants such as cotton lavender have been allowed to go woody at the base over time and clipped into interesting forms.

unbowed in his convictions about what is right for the space. 'This is a garden that has grown out of the landscape. Derek established a clear vocabulary of materials with the driftwood, rusted metal, the stones at the front of the garden – "these large dragon teeth flints", as he described them.

'Understanding that frame allows you to do a lot within it. Keith was gentle in his stewardship, but he did make creative interventions in the garden. It's important to allow it to change.' Jonny has put time into cultivating relationships with the residents of Dungeness, just as Keith did, and now they often call him to collect an old groyne or weatherbeaten piece they have pulled up in their fishing nets, to use in the garden just as Jarman did.

ABOVE Stone-edged beds in the shingle host red valerian, California poppies, red poppies, lavender, marjoram and salvias. **FACING PAGE** Derek Jarman and Keith Collins made sculptures and works from the jetsam they found on the beach, from pieces of metal and stones to driftwood. **OVERLEAF** Jonny tending his stock beds on his own nursery, The Field, in the Cotswolds.

Horticulture has moved on since the 1990s, and dry gardens and those using native plants are now more accepted, tested and embraced. Inspired by innovators like Peter Korn in Sweden, Jonny now sows and grows all the plants intended for the garden in sand beds, so they are more resilient to the challenging conditions.

It looms large in his life, but Jonny only spends one weekend a month working at Prospect. His is a peripatetic practice of many facets, from growing and freelance gardening to botanical illustration. While training at Aberglasney in West Wales and during his two-year scholarship at Great Dixter in East Sussex, he created a hand-printed zine called *The Germ* concerned with the exploration of nature, and he still writes regularly about plants, places and the craft of gardening for various publications.

But it was while he was at Dixter that the seeds of his future life were sown. The garden hosts two well-loved plant fairs each year, and it was here that Jonny met Hans and Miranda Kramer of De Hessenhof nursery in the Netherlands. 'They were the first nursery I'd ever seen with the organic certification label. They were growing in leaf mould and they had plants I'd never seen before – it was very exciting.'

At the end of his Dixter placement, looking for work, he reached out the Kramers and went to Hessenhof with the idea of doing a three-month internship. 'I ended up staying there for almost five years.' The nursery has an unusually large collection of more than 6,000 varieties of perennial plants, which are all grown organically, and from which around 3,000 plants are propagated annually. 'That was an eye-opening experience – to see what was possible, rather than relying on bought-in material.'

Hans and Miranda became Jonny's friends as well as his employers, gifting him a puppy and generally making him feel wanted and valued. 'They gave me my freedom. It was clear that they saw my potential. I turned up at Hessenhof with pockets full of seed from Dixter, wanting to grow all these things, and Hans said, "I think you need your own garden." The next day, he dug up half the car park, gave me a big area and said, "This is yours."'

For the next four years, Jonny made an experimental garden in his car-park patch, composing schemes with a Dixter approach, but using the new palette of plants he found at Hessenhof. 'It was formative, and I was so grateful. Those two things they did for me – giving me my dog Frida and my own garden – were so powerful.'

While there, Jonny also became friends with the legendary planting designer Piet Oudolf and his wife, Anya, who live near the nursery, and often bring plant-loving guests to visit and see Hans's mother beds – the stock plants from which all others come. Piet gave Jonny a tour of his own garden at Hummelo, and was impressed with Jonny's knowledge of and passion for plants. He has since become a champion for Jonny, asking for him to compere public talks and write an essay for a book about his life.

Working at Hessenhof made Jonny reconsider what his next steps and long-term plan should be, shifting from garden making fully into plant husbandry with a new dream of running his own nursery. 'It was probably in my third year there that I realized that this is the life that I want, not just a means to an end. That's when I started looking for land. It took a long time to find it.'

After many years Jonny finally found an empty plot near Cirencester, right in the centre of the Cotswolds, attached to a new housing estate. He had to persuade the developer to hand it over and the local council to give planning permission, but in 2025 he and his right-hand man Daniel Carlson plus a motley crew of family and friends began building the infrastructure from scratch. They planted stock beds, constructed a potting shed and started the long process of propagating all the plants they want to sell.

It's just the beginning for The Field Nursery, as Jonny decided to call it, and although he has plans for a garden and an education hub, he is aware this is something that has to develop slowly. 'There's a poetry in allowing things to grow naturally,' he says. 'We're in no rush. Having this opportunity to live out a long-held dream is an exceptional thing, so there's a lot of time to build the nursery into something special.'

FACING Derek was captured on camera gardening in a boiler suit and Jonny continues the tradition as caretaker of this special place.

DECLAN BUCKLEY

'EVERYTHING IN THIS garden gets way taller than it's supposed to,' says Declan Buckley, looking up at a towering brassaiopsis which obviously hasn't read the plant books. The garden designer, who was previously an art director and graphic designer, has been developing this Bali-inspired tropical paradise in north London over the past two decades. Giant, large-leaved plants abound, from fatsia and tetrapanax to Dicksonia tree ferns and scheffleras, and the cool shade of their jungly canopy creates an enticing sense of mystery.

Even as a child growing up in Co. Cork, Ireland, Declan had a plant obsession. Having wangled his own greenhouse out of his father, he grew and propagated unusual exotic things such as cacti and palms, and pestered the women at a local nursery every weekend to teach him more about plants. 'They were totally surprised when I didn't go on to study horticulture. But at that time, you had to go to agricultural college first.' As a gay teenager in Ireland in the 1970s, the idea of spending a year with a bunch of farmers in a rural college was not an attractive prospect.

Declan ended up coming to the UK aged seventeen to study architecture in Huddersfield, but that didn't last long for various reasons, from bouts of glandular fever to a distinct lack of interest in the teaching approach. 'In the first term, we learned about the freezing points of different concrete,' he explains. 'It just wasn't for me.'

Back home in Ireland, he tried to break into the world of graphic design and advertising. 'I couldn't drive, but I got a job as a motorbike messenger for an agency. Then I went out and bought a motorbike.' Several crashes later, it was a relief to move into working in the photography darkroom instead.

After his grandmother died and left him some money, he was able to fulfil his dream of going to art school, and soon after he started up a design studio creating graphics, posters and leaflets for theatres, art galleries and advocacy groups in Dublin. At that time, posters were a vibrant format to work in – not only a successful medium for advertising but also a powerful, democratic art form, vital for grassroots movements, and a vehicle for expression and social commentary.

Declan had been working on a series around the abortion referendum in Ireland and women's right to choose – 'then a lost cause,' he says – before leaving the country again to join an ad agency in San Francisco, where he specialized in campaigns around issues such as reproductive rights and environmentalism.

By the time he returned to London, the HIV/AIDS pandemic was at its peak. He got involved with a group called Gay Men Fighting AIDS (GMFA) – now known as LGBT HERO – helping to create their corporate identity as well as posters and TV ads. 'We made the first series of safe-sex ads for gay men in the world. They were cheeky, and sexy, but then they were banned by the Advertising Standards Authority because they came too close to Section 28.'

This legislation, which was in force between 1988 and 2003, prohibited the promotion or endorsement of homosexuality in a positive light, or at all, by local authorities. 'But Channel 4 pushed back and put the ads within the TV programme rather than on advertising time, so they got aired.' Declan recently discovered that twenty-five pieces of his work for GMFA are now held in the permanent collection of the V&A.

'I ended up doing lots of work around that, but it's difficult when all your friends are dying. I got burnt out by the whole thing,' admits Declan. It was around this time that he

reconnected with his love of gardening, creating a small roof garden for his old flat, with layers of green in containers and pots. 'Everything had to really earn its keep on that tiny little terrace. The plants were the least of it – you had to get the pots up there and then the soil, and then finally put the plant in it. And it needed so much watering.'

A pivotal moment came when he entered it into a local garden competition in 1998, judged by designer Dan Pearson, and won. He decided to study horticulture and garden design part time, gradually building up a client base. 'I would go and see clients to drop off book covers and things, and they'd ask what I was doing, so I told them. And they'd say, "Oh, we've just bought a house. Would you mind designing our garden for us?" So it developed naturally from there.'

Since then, he has got to work on projects he'd never have dreamed of, from large-scale landscapes in India to gardens in Lithuania and Armenia, and rewilding an old pig farm in Ireland

ABOVE A bridge across the pond leads into a tiny jungle of subtropical greenery. **FACING, CLOCKWISE FROM TOP LEFT** A modern glass galleria looks down over the patio outside the back door. It is overhung with star jasmine, which creates a curtain to screen the outdoor shower here; koi named after the royal family and waterlilies are at home in fountain-fed pool; long, bent limbs of scheffleras and other exotic plants cross the path; Declan's ceramic sculptures appear throughout the space.

before rewilding had a name. But his bread and butter has always been small London gardens, of which he has created many, and his own city plot has played a major role in bringing him this work.

Like many British back gardens, it is long and skinny – about 23 metres (75 feet) long by 7 metres (23 feet) wide – and was completely overlooked when Declan first arrived. 'I had lots of five-storey houses looking down on me. It felt like you were in a football stadium, because there was just a wall of windows. So privacy was the first thing I wanted to create.'

Many of the plants Declan had chosen to grow on his former roof terrace originated from New Zealand, and trips there and to Bali to see plants growing in the wild were a huge influence on the character and style of his new space.

'I loved the idea of being in the treetops. It's taken close to twenty years for that to happen but now it feels like I'm living in a tree house.' The first impression, looking down from the first floor through full-length glass, is of verdant abundance, with most of the garden completely hidden from view behind a mass of green foliage.

'All of the houses here had what I call original Victorian gallerias,' says Declan, referring to the tiny first-floor conservatory spaces that are common in his area. 'I had some architect friends design a modern glass box version for me so you could be in the house and the garden at the same time.'

Downstairs, as you step outside, you find Declan's *pièce de résistance* tucked in under a bower of false jasmine: a secret outdoor shower, a brilliant indulgence. 'You can have a hot shower in the morning in the garden – even in the middle of winter, we use it all the time.'

The black-painted, ivy-clad boundaries of the garden aid the feeling of immersion and enclosure. Further along, past a cluster of pots filled with ferns and a maidenhair vine, a wall fountain with three spouts feeds into a rectangular pool. The sound of the water sploshing down blissfully covers the ambient noise of the urban setting. Streaks of orange flash beneath the surface – a glint of golden orfe.

A timber bridge leads over the water to a dark slate path, blocked by gangly, twisted tree limbs you have to duck under. Beneath, shade-loving ground-cover plants including ferns and more unusual specimens such as *Disporopsis taiwanensis* and a Japanese form of *Reineckea carnea* fill in the understorey. At the end of the garden is a lighter, brighter terrace with a large metal table and chairs for entertaining on warm evenings.

Though he moves some tender houseplants out to the garden in summer, the mildness of the city winters and cover of the dense planting here creates a microclimate that allows Declan to grow some borderline things outside all year. Most of his stock are hardy plants that look subtropical, but he likes to push the limits occasionally, and this space has acted as a helpful testing ground for him to experiment with plants before using them in client projects.

The garden has had lots of publicity over the years, which Declan is at once delighted and annoyed by. When every client wants a version of your own garden, he explains, it starts to feel like you've been typecast. But even when he is using a completely different plant palette, his style is always focused on structural, textural planting and creating a memorable atmosphere – something that stays with people.

'I had a lovely message from someone studying garden design who had been inspired by the garden I designed for their father years and years before. I thought that was really sweet – you design a garden for somebody and years later their son has taken up garden design because of it.'

After twenty-five years in practice, however, Declan is now slowing down and only taking on a few projects with established clients. These days, he is more interested in working on a fresh passion – ceramics, which offers a creative freedom that is utterly new to him. 'For fifty years, I've been working to somebody else's brief,' he says. 'So it was quite terrifying taking up ceramics because nobody is telling me what to do and there are no boundaries.'

He did briefly attempt using a pottery wheel – 'I can't throw to save my life, and after an hour in front of a wheel, I'm screaming for an osteopath' – but mostly hand-builds his sculptural vessels in a freeform way.

His works are organic rather than geometric, and are heavily influenced by nature. 'I might start off with a walk in the garden in the morning, and collect some twigs or seed pods that I either emboss or use as tools on the clay. And that will take things in a particular direction. I work a lot with texture and it's almost like collage, cutting out, sticking on things and building things up. Just like in my gardens, I'm more interested in texture than colour.'

He has had a couple of gallery exhibitions and been asked to do commissions, but the biggest collection of his work is on show in his home and in the garden, where sculptures of stacked, texturized black tubes perfectly mimic the bare trunks of his crown-raised trees.

It may be thousands of miles from the sultry island that inspired it, but this hybrid haven of hardy exotics is Declan's natural habitat. 'I think I wouldn't be able to cope in London without having a garden like this,' he says. 'It's like getting lost in your own little world.'

FACING Past huge pots of *Cautleya spicata* 'Arun Flame', there is a dining set on the terrace at the end of the garden, with Declan's ceramic bowls on display on the table.

CHARLIE HARPUR

CHARLIE HARPUR lies awake at night worrying about what is working and what isn't in the garden at Knepp. 'It's very different to being a head gardener somewhere else,' he says. 'The best thing is having a green light to experiment and the freedom to push boundaries. But there is a pressure that comes with that.'

The 1,416 hectare (3,500 acre) estate was famously taken out of conventional farming in the early 2000s by owners Charles Burrell and Isabella Tree, who embarked on a pioneering nature conservation plan to turn it into a biodiverse wilderness area. They allowed native vegetation to re-establish and brought in animals such as fallow deer, old English longhorn cattle, Tamworth pigs and Exmoor ponies to roam free, graze, rootle and cause disturbance. They also attempted to introduce beavers and were successful in introducing white storks. Wildlife has increased massively in response to the resulting mosaic of habitats, with many threatened or rare types of bird and insect showing up in subsequent biodiversity audits and surveys.

At the heart of the estate, however, around the family home of Knepp Castle, there was a slightly embarrassing, incongruous outlier – the 0.4 hectare (1 acre) walled garden, split in two with a kitchen garden on one side and a flat croquet lawn and swimming pool on the other. It was not giving 'rewilding'. But how on earth, the Burrells wondered, would you rewild a garden anyway? To answer that question, they formed a garden advisory board with landscape designer Tom Stuart-Smith, botanist Mick Crawley, planting designer James Hitchmough and grower Jekka McVicar.

'The goal for the whole project was maximum biodiversity within the garden,' says Charlie. 'Everything else is kind of a by-product. People get really wound up by the term "rewilding", and obsessed about terminology, so we have to explain that we've taken a scientific definition and adapted it. It is rewilding in the sense that it is mimicking natural processes and creating a kaleidoscope of different habitats. It's just that the smaller the area you are dealing with, the more that the human – the gardener – has to adapt to and mimic.'

Charlie has always had links to the horticultural world, as his grandfather Jerry and uncle Marcus were both lauded garden photographers, but he started out in architecture, studying in Bath and doing placements in studios such as Ted Cullinan's in London, before heading to Sweden to do his masters degree. There, stuck behind a screen and thoroughly disenchanted, he finally admitted to himself that he didn't want to pursue it as a career.

In 2013, he wrote to Tom Stuart-Smith to ask for a job in his landscape studio, but there was no spot available. Tom relented a few weeks later, however, and offered Charlie an internship. 'So I dropped everything to come back, and ended up staying for three years, doing a lot of architectural detailing, before picking up more on the planting side and getting my own projects.'

Throughout all of this, Charlie was experiencing mental health issues. He speaks candidly about battling depression at different times and believes that two things saved his life: gardening and running (he regularly takes part in marathons and ultra-marathons, as an individual and on teams, and is a British 100km and UK trail-running champion).

Growing and working with plants was increasingly important for him, so he went back to train at the Chelsea Physic Garden and then did the Kew Diploma. Along the way he volunteered at interesting gardens, from Fulham Palace to

Villa Boccanegra in Italy, as well as growing his own produce on the tiny rooftop of his London flat.

He was just finishing his dissertation on ecological gardening and unsure what his next step might be when Tom got in touch again to tempt him back to work on an exciting new venture: establishing a 'library' of plants at Tom's home ground of Serge Hill in Hertfordshire.

Originally conceived as a reference resource for his design team, this collection of more than 1,200 plants is now a popular draw for horticulture students, professional designers and gardeners and others keen to observe how different species and cultivars of perennial plants grow over the seasons and years.

The master plan for the Knepp project was on the drawing board in the studio, and Charlie was intrigued by the idea of rewilding a garden. Such a highly experimental project was a step into the unknown for all involved – 'Tom called it a box of unpredictabilities' – because once the concept had been decided and initial planting went in, no one really knew where the garden would take them.

The Burrells were looking for someone to come on board to oversee its establishment phase and further development, as well as input to the creation of a market garden for their new farm shop and café. Charlie couldn't resist the opportunity, and in spring 2022 joined the existing team of gardeners, who had already implemented the design for the walled garden.

In the rewilded garden, this involved creating a new topography of mounds, ridges and dips using 400 tonnes of crushed-up remains of an old farm building, mixed with sand and gravel, to create a brownfield-inspired, free-draining substrate. Tom specified a tapestry of plants and James Hitchmough created a tailored seed mix to sow along the central ridge, creating a low-input, drought-tolerant,

PREVIOUS Charlie in the Rewilded Garden in the Walled Garden, where 'volunteer' plants such as willow and butterfly bushes vie for space with late-summer flowering perennials. The bug stack creates a focal point as well as habitat with layers of cut down material between stout hazel poles. **ABOVE** In the Kitchen Garden, beds of vegetables and 'edimentals', such as rose hips, surround the old Victorian well. **FACING** Gardening here is all about building habitat, from piles of sand to bug hotels and piles of lying dead wood alongside the old brick walls filled with nooks and crannies.

climate-resilient planting it was hoped would attract more bees, butterflies, beetles and bugs. The old kitchen garden was not landscaped but instead left to loosen up a little, with self-seeders allowed to 'dirty' the paths and yew forms being 'goat-pruned' rather than topiarized.

'Tom said that he's never felt with any other project more than Knepp that he was just setting the stage, and kickstarting processes to see what happened,' says Charlie. 'Then it would be us, the gardeners, that steer it. He comes back often to check in, but we're sort of on our own, and that's what makes it quite interesting. And it has thrown up some surprises for us about what it means to take it forward, and figuring out how we react to what happens.'

This is gardening as ongoing curation, rather than maintaining a space with a specific set of aesthetic goals. It provides Charlie and the team with, depending on how you look at it, a gratifying and/or terrifying amount of autonomy. Take, for example, the landscape succession drama playing out with pioneer shrubs including gorse, birch and willow, which have popped up on their own. They weren't part of the original planting, but now they are there, should they be removed? What benefits might they bring if left to their own devices or managed in some way? It is these and countless other decisions that the team must make every day as the seasons and years roll on.

To help, Charlie has developed what he calls 'the grazing index', a list of all the plants that have turned up in the garden with information about the roles they could play. 'It's not a complete guide, but it gives you a pretty good idea of the different ecosystem services plants can provide, from deep taproots breaking up clay, edible plants and plants that soak up water. Does it look good? Does it get invasive and spread? Does it function as a good garden plant? Does it smell nice? Those are some of our grazing index criteria that then give us a total score per plant, so when we are roaming through an area of planting, we can make split-second decisions on what stays and what goes, based on the role something can play for wildlife and the ecosystem.'

'We're making a web of complexity that we didn't have before. That is our remit as gardeners.'

FACING Tall vertical evergreen cypress disrupt the naturalistic swathes of *Stipa gigantea* grass and understorey of echinacea, euphorbia and buddleja. **ABOVE** At one end, a pergola offers a shady place to sit for the family – this is still their private garden.

Charlie has also been adding more structural complexity, such as his 'lumpy-bumpy bits' – piles of sand dotted around the garden's sunny spots to mimic ant hills or termite mounds. 'The building rubble substrate was good for growing plants, but not as great for burrowing insects,' he explains. 'Adding sand opened the garden up to a lot of insects, and has proved amazingly successful. Watching the piles now, it's like a whole David Attenborough documentary playing out. We're making a web of complexity that we didn't have before. That is our remit as gardeners, as the keystone species here, to continue.'

Another addition is the new pergola-like structure built out of stag's head oaks – the dead, antler-like limbs that form in the tops of old tree canopies – into which Charlie drilled holes to provide homes for different insects. 'Within forty-five minutes we had solitary wasps sizing up the apertures – I still had the drill out.'

All sorts of seasonal tasks are approached in a novel way too. 'Our cutting back is actually an artistic process. Rather than getting the hedge trimmer out, cutting it all back, taking the material away and mulching, what we do is we chip away at it for a long time, a bit here and a bit there, so you get a good distribution of plants left standing. We see ourselves as herbivores that go in and nibble away at it, rather than mowing everything to the ground.'

They also cut plants down at various levels for different species to inhabit. 'If they've got pithy or hollow stems, for example, we cut them at what we call beaver height, where a beaver would fell a tree. Other plants we don't cut back at all, so they're still standing in May with their dead seed heads displayed. It gives a good balance of decay to new life.'

This acceptance of gone over and dead vegetation, it turns out, is the most challenging aspect of the Knepp approach, even for its team, who know the importance of decaying matter for biodiversity. We may now, thanks to the gospel of Dutch Wave maestro Piet Oudolf, be able to appreciate frosted seed heads over winter, but are we as willing to accept brown bits in spring, or even summer? 'As gardeners, we generally see death as a failure,' says Charlie. 'We are all trained horticulturists and actually very tidy gardeners here, so it's hard sometimes to change the way you think and approach things.'

The key to combatting the discomfort, for themselves, the Burrell family (whose private home garden this still is) and the legions of curious visitors who come for a nosey on garden safaris to see what all the fuss is about – is 'cues to care'. This phrase was coined by landscape architect Joan Nassauer in her pivotal paper 'Messy Ecosystems, Orderly Frames'. It describes how naturalistic spaces are made more acceptable to us through obvious indications that the landscape is intentional and cared for, such as a path mown through a meadow.

'It's the neglect that people perceive in wild-looking spaces which makes them really stressed, because they will assume that an area is out of control and has been abandoned,' says Charlie. 'We don't connect well to those kind of spaces. You need to show people that it is being looked after, and that is the thing that requires a lot of artistic intervention.'

He points out the spontaneous, bird-seeded roses that have turned up around the kitchen garden, and which the team graze or contort into interesting shapes, or even use to tie up floppy perennials. 'And when it comes to things like hemerocallis and irises that have a lot of wispy foliage that doesn't decay as beautifully, and sprawls and covers everything, we'll curate it to make little nests around each plant.'

Rewilding the garden has never been about just letting it go to do whatever it wants with no intervention – though many people seem to think this before they come and see for themselves. Charlie knows all too well that in this role he is working on hearts and minds as well as the garden itself. 'So I lie in bed awake wondering, "What are people going to think?" I still have a great fear of failure, even though I know that's a vital part of it. All of this is to enact a sort of crazy dream that might work, but might not. There's no fixed answer. It's an experiment. But at least we're giving it a go.'

FACING Charlie and the team introduced these stag horn oak branches as sculptural standing dead wood – quickly populated by solitary wasps.

KAORI TATEBAYASHI

ONE BISQUE-COLOURED BRANCH laden with magnolia flowers. Hollyhock stems in bud and bloom in a haunting shade of pale. A ghostly garden growing out of a gallery wall. Even stepping closer does not dispel the illusion, because every petal, every leaf marking is so perfectly real. These extraordinary pieces, created by Japanese artist Kaori Tatebayashi, seem to capture the very essence, the soul of these plants.

The care and love she has for them shine out of every corner of her studio in Deptford, where wraithlike ivy climbs the wall and handmade reproductions of poppies, peonies, lilies and tulips line the trestle table where she works.

Kaori was born in the town of Arita, famous for its porcelain, but her family moved to Kyoto when she was five. She always loved drawing and being creative, so went to a specialist high school for art and design, where tutors spotted her skill in creating 3D forms.

She trained in traditional pottery techniques at university, such as throwing and hand modelling, but was also able to experiment. 'I tried textiles, Japanese lacquer and ceramics,' she says, 'and ceramics was the one that was closest to my heart.' In Japan, the discipline is still dominated by functional ceramics – vessels. But there was a movement that began in Kyoto in the 1950s, called Sōdeisha, where a group of avant-garde artists started creating forms with no function – ceramic sculpture, or what was called Object ceramics.

The artist Yō Akiyama, who is considered a late proponent of the movement, was also, luckily, Kaori's professor, so she had his example and guidance as she set about exploring what else the clay could become and do. The issue for her was the final surface finish. 'Back then, ceramics always had a hard, heavy glaze, and I didn't feel that was necessary; I wanted to remove it so you could just see the form.'

She credits a visiting exhibition of contemporary British ceramics as life changing. 'It was mostly sculptural work, and they didn't have this shiny, heavy glaze.' As well as being inspired by this new work in clay, she was keen to learn slab building, which was more common in the UK, so she applied for an exchange programme with the Royal College of Art, and got it. Kaori came to London for one term. 'Everything was so crazy and fresh,' she says. 'During that time, I made sculpture and explored different finishes, still searching for the right sort of surface for my work.'

Kaori returned to London several years later to forge her career, teaching and making tableware and sculptural pieces. She found the European manmade clay more controllable than what she had worked with in Japan, and developed a central theme of freezing time in her work. 'I realized that's something ceramics can do that maybe no other medium can. I wanted to enhance that feeling that time is trapped within the object. But stopping the clock with a still-life object doesn't give such a strong sense of capturing a moment, so my subjects changed to small insects and plants.'

Her final breakthrough came soon after. 'One day I realized that the surface actually doesn't need any glaze; I can just leave the clay once-fired. It was like a revolution for me. At that point I made the decision to leave the glaze out completely from my work.'

The first flower she made in clay was a hyacinth. 'It was a surprise – I had thought that making flowers and plants in clay wasn't possible, but then the hyacinth was successful and I thought, okay, maybe I can do this. Around the same time, I

became passionate about gardening, so that influenced me a lot. Being in the garden really inspires me.'

Her only growing space back then was the front garden of her flat – a communal space with no garden to speak of aside from a few trees. 'It was my first garden, so I was really excited. I started adding plants, but I was a total beginner. It has very heavy clay soil, and I just randomly added plants that I wanted and not what suited the conditions, so most of them disappeared or didn't come back. But slowly I learned. Now it is quite a mature garden, and I'm very happy with it.'

Fifteen years on, she is still the only one who gardens there, but her neighbours are all appreciative. 'It's not a big garden, but to do it on my own, it's big enough; it's a handful. The residents have changed over the years, but some tell me they bought their flats because they love the garden, so I think it's in everyone's favour. I get occasional bottles of wine to say thank you.'

In the garden, Kaori has plenty of shrubs to give it some structure, lots of perennials, roses and tough plants like her fig tree. 'I love combining shapes and forms and different greens, and any flowers are an addition to that.'

She also has an allotment where she experiments with natural farming methods, and grows flowers that wouldn't thrive in the garden. 'I grow broad beans and French beans and potatoes. The carrots were a total failure, and my tomatoes didn't do very well, but I have grown delicious aubergines. There's peppers, peas and chard, daikon, radish and pumpkins, as well as sweetcorn – I ate one cob raw, it was so sweet.'

Blooms here include dahlias, foxgloves, sweet peas and French marigolds. 'Another thing I can't grow in the garden is irises, and I really need bearded irises for my work, so I have planted some rhizomes at the allotment to see if they will do well there.'

Ideally, she says, she'd love to grow everything she models, but it's not always possible. 'I borrow plants from my friends' gardens or sometimes buy them from a plant nursery. But I

ABOVE LEFT In Kaori's garden, which she tends alone but shares with other residents of her building, she grows flowers including verbascum and nasturtiums. **ABOVE RIGHT** As an artist she is always observing the form of plants, such as this day lily, to see if they might make good subjects for her work. **FACING** Kaori on the front steps of her apartment building, surrounded by her pots of herbs, fruit and flowers as well as shrubs and flowering perennials she has planted.

143

'I actually love brambles because they grow with a real freeness of form, climbing up or spreading with arched stems.'

prefer the wild forms of plants to heavily cultivated varieties – often nursery plants are too well behaved, and don't have as much impact on me as when I encounter them in nature or the garden. They don't have many imperfections, which in nature are always there. I need those imperfections in my models. It makes the plant look super realistic.'

Although it looks like she makes quite a big range of plants and flowers, they are actually very carefully selected. She likes flowers that have thick stems and bulky leaves, such as foxgloves. 'There are a lot of plants that are difficult to do in clay. Dandelion fluff is impossible, as are umbels like cow parsley, and also rose leaves.'

She always brings the flower she wishes to model into her studio. 'I never work from photographs or memory. I need the actual plant in front of me. Usually, it's a plant in a pot, because it will last longer; it's quite difficult to work from cut stems because you have to work very fast.' Sometimes she has to collect plants or cut flowers from clients' own gardens and dash back to her studio to recreate them, even keeping some in the fridge overnight to prolong their lives.

Amazingly, Kaori's skill is such that she does not make any preliminary drawings, but starts directly making in clay. 'They're almost like clay sketches,' she says. 'I just grab a piece of clay and observe the model, and decide what sort of technique I can use. For the stem, I would probably use the same sort of movement as pulling handles for cups; for a round form, I would use a coiling technique and a little bit of slab building and modelling.'

She has to work quickly to avoid the clay drying, so she builds in small sections, creating directly on the kiln shelf, supporting delicate pieces as she goes with nuggets of fired clay. 'When I start a section, I have to finish it in the same day. I don't carry on with the same section the next day, because one thing I can never do is to spray water on to my clay.'

PREVIOUS Kaori's allotment gives her the opportunity to grow food inspired by the natural farming movement. **FACING, CLOCKWISE FROM TOP** In her studio, Kaori works from real-life plant models using her hands and simple clay modelling tools, creating beautiful unglazed pieces representing everything from weeds and birds to magnolia flowers and pine cones.

Kaori fires the different sections in her kiln, and then brings her pieces together at the point of installation. Blooms and leaflets are assembled on the wall, with the joints carefully hidden beneath the flowerheads or leaves, making the installation seamless. 'The fragility of my work is the biggest challenge, and installing them is the most nerve-wracking part. I have to fully concentrate; otherwise, I start to think too much about what would happen if I dropped a piece, and my hands start to shake.'

Previous works have ranged from individual stems to more complex compositions of different plants and flowers, which Kaori ensures are horticulturally accurate. 'I don't mix spring flowers with autumn ones, for example, because as a scene, it doesn't look right; because I know that doesn't happen in real life. I want my work to be true to nature in every way.'

The finished pieces are breathtaking, but for Kaori it's not just about the end result. For her, modelling certain plants feels like she's connecting with and making a portrait of an individual, not just capturing their looks when they are fully in bloom. 'To watch them from when they are just seeds germinating, and through growing, helps me to understand them and their anatomy. When I am monitoring them, I am getting to know them, and once I have made the piece, I feel like I know them very well.'

She is on a constant search for new models, and she often finds her next subject by visiting gardens – though there is also a fair amount of foraging in her practice. Kaori is also not adverse to including portrayals of gardeners' most hated weeds in her work, regularly featuring bindweed twining up a stem or a dandelion flower in bud.

'I actually love brambles because they grow with a real freeness of form, climbing up or spreading with arched stems. But what I like most about them is that they're available all through the year, so even in February when there is nothing else to model, there are always brambles,' she says. 'The park next door is bramble heaven, and unlike the flowers, no one minds if I cut some brambles!'

CO. WICKLOW, IRELAND

JIMI BLAKE

WALKING THROUGH HUNTING BROOK Gardens, everywhere you look there are plants you can't name, like a jet-black agapanthus, furry cacti and crooked-limbed conifers. There are also ones you think you might recognize, but are way bigger than you've ever seen before.

Its creator, Jimi Blake, is proud to be prince of the plant nerds, addicted to collecting all types. 'I'm always making lists,' he says. 'My most enjoyable thing is to go out and make lists of snowdrops or figure out how many epimediums I have. The higher the number, the more of a high I get.'

He started this extraordinary garden, by the Wicklow Mountains in Ireland, from scratch more than twenty years ago, and has constantly evolved it ever since. In the early years, it comprised simply borders lining the drive to his small cabin-like home, the beds packed with plant-hunted hardy exotics from an expedition to China. There was an Oudolf-inflected grasses phase and a tropical fling with tender gingers and bananas, but it's the woodland plants that own his heart these days, as the trees he planted all those years ago mature and the surrounding woods encroach more and more.

Jimi grew up right here on the family farm, but didn't like farming much. 'My father was tough and we had to work hard as little kids. We had a huge garden, and it became my escape, because I loved being with my mother. Gardening with her was a lovely experience. She always had little projects going on.'

They had a small polytunnel that Jimi considered a safe space, where he could propagate cuttings and sow seeds. 'We had a rickety old lean-to glasshouse as well. I was so excited to get a paraffin heater for in there, but one night I put petrol into it instead of paraffin, and blew up the glasshouse. The whole thing caught fire, and our house nearly burnt down.'

Despite this setback, Jimi's burgeoning passion for plants continued to develop. As he grew up, school was particularly difficult, and gardening became his only outlet. A teacher took notice of his interest and helped him look for further training, so straight after school he found himself studying amenity horticulture at the National Botanic Gardens of Ireland in Dublin. 'That was a big leap for me, and one of the major turning points in my life. Suddenly I was away from home, surrounded by people that loved plants as much as me.'

As part of the course, Jimi was sent to do work placements at different parks. 'It was brutal: raking leaves, planting motorway hedges, litterpicking and rounding up wild horses. The parks can wear you down. But then I got transferred to the nursery at St Anne's Park in Raheny, doing propagation with Ed Bowden, who became a really good friend. I was just coming out at the time and he was out already, and I looked up to him on that side of things as well as in horticulture.'

Jimi went on to do the rounds maintaining private gardens for a while, which he hated, before being offered a role at Airfield, an overgrown walled garden that was part of an old estate in Dundrum, south Dublin. 'I was only about twenty-two, and I was still learning, but I was head gardener, and really the only gardener for a while. The whole garden had to be restored. I lived in the gate lodge and although it was in town, it felt like the country. It was a magic time.' The well-known Irish gardener and presenter Helen Dillon had her TV garden on site too, and everyone was keen to develop the garden and open it to the public.

Jimi was there for more than a decade, and over the years built a team and started teaching courses. He created new

PREVIOUS The borders that line the path at the garden's entrance are an explosion of colour and texture with bright dahlias and rose campion alongside spears of *Pseudopanax ferox* and towering aralia. **FACING TOP** The woodland beds are Jimi's passion and are packed with interesting shrubs and lower-storey shade-loving plants. **FACING BOTTOM** Hunting Brook has diverse areas with eclectic plant displays, including old agricultural feed troughs filled with furry cacti and tables topped with pots of interesting succulents and tender plants. **ABOVE** Outside Jimi's log-cabin-style house lie his greenhouse and sand beds.

borders, grew the plant collections and travelled to see other gardens, meet gardeners and visit plant fairs. But there was a pull to go back home, with the offer of taking on 8 hectares (20 acres) of the farm as his own.

He had no idea how he would make a living, but made the decision to just go for it, building his little house and rushing desperately to make a new garden in time for opening to visitors the next summer. 'The garden scene in Ireland was really just taking off, but I had a lot of support from the older garden community that I knew from going to horticultural meetings.'

At first there was just one border lining the driveway, but over the years Jimi expanded the planting, as and when he could, with new beds and areas, usually with all home-propagated plants. Now, when you arrive at Hunting Brook, it is up a slim, sloping path into a wonderland of colourful flowers and interesting shrubs, where jewel-toned dahlias jostle with skinny spires of lancewood (pseudopanax) and tall aralias. 'I wanted that feeling when you enter that you are in a completely different world,' he says.

Jimi has been collecting the seed of single dahlias for several years now and is ready to name some choice selections, including a clear red bloom for his mother, Kathleen. For him, however, it is about the foliage plants just as much as the flowers, with a backdrop of large schefflera, big rhododendrons and stands of bamboo.

In front of the house, they frame new mounded island beds that contain diverse and surprising combinations. On my visit, one featured an arresting display of white-haired cacti standing erect among purple-leaved plants and hot-coloured blooms such as red echinaceas and orange poppies. Another bed held the vertical accents of bobbly conifers with outstretched arms, underplanted with bright blue salvias and silver leaves.

'I'm getting into evergreens,' explains Jimi. 'In this climate, I have to cut back the perennial borders for winter or it all goes slimy and sloppy, but then I need something to look at. I have twenty-five different conifers in this area of the garden so there is structure, and that's definitely the direction I'm going in. I love playing with that quirkiness – they're going to be like sculptures.'

Further along are his experimental sand beds, and then wrapping around the rest of the house, down to the woods, are several woodland beds. This is where he has his collections, including epimediums, corydalis and more than eight hundred types of snowdrop. 'They give me an incredibly long season. When I get up in the morning, I go out to the woodland beds, because that's where the interest is.'

He has started working on some more beds down into the woodland itself, trying a no-dig method. It's part of his mission to change his approach. 'I know I am letting the garden get too big, but the newer areas are much easier to look after. The big borders are the ones that keep changing. But do I really want to be digging up dahlias for the rest of my life, and is it the right way to garden? They are so much work. You're constantly disturbing the soil, and it doesn't sit right with me anymore that you're left with bare soil in winter. It's not the way I want to garden.'

LEFT At the bottom of the woodland valley there is a stream surrounded by lush planting. **FACING** The moss-covered table is a gathering spot for Jimi's visitors and volunteers, surrounded by ferns, bamboo and many of his rare and exciting woodland plants.

'I am always thinking about the design, the combinations, the flow, the textures, everything.'

ABOVE The meadow at Hunting Brook offers a wide-open space after being deep in the woods, and offers views of the Wicklow Mountains.

Jimi is also reconsidering the tender plants he uses, giving many of his aeoniums, banana plants and cacti to a neighbour for their conservatory for the winter. 'I feel like I am punishing a poor plant that just has two months outside and is trapped inside the rest of the time. I would really like to scale that back. I do love putting those white cacti somewhere new every year, though – that kind of plays with people's minds.'

He loves having these striking, sometimes clashing notes within his planting design, admitting that he likes to always have a bit of 'bonkers stuff' to stop people in their tracks. 'I am always thinking about the design, the combinations, the flow, the textures, everything. And when I'm in that creative space, I feel a really deep alignment with who I am. It's very grounding. If I was just to maintain the garden as it is, that would absolutely bore me to tears. If you just cut back everything every year, keep the status quo, then you're not dealing with anything or being creative. It's the same in life. If we don't deal with stuff, we don't evolve. I need to keep that excitement about plants going.'

At the edge of the garden is a sign declaring the route down to the woodland valley. Here, under a towering ceiling of larch, sycamore, beech and a few oaks, Jimi has cut routes and steps into the steep sides so you can traverse the slopes and enjoy his introductions of leafy shrubs including magnificent magnolias and scheffleras.

Although the ravine recalls a flavour of some Cornish gardens and there are notes of more traditional woodland walks, this is a contemporary take on the form. The quiet, winding paths twist and turn. Birds call and water drips off leaves. Rays of sunlight reach down through the high canopy. Brushing past exotic-looking treasures, you could be in a rainforest and not beside farmland in County Wicklow. Down, down you go, all the way to a bridge over a babbling stream, and a haunting old table taken over by moss.

'The valley is the most special part of Hunting Brook,' explains Jimi. 'All the fuss is at the top, but the valley is almost like a sacred space. I don't come down here thinking I have to do a million things. It's a beautiful place.'

Back up the other side of the valley, you venture out of the peaceful embrace of the woods into an open, sunny meadow with a view of the distant mountains. There are wild flowers including thousands of orchids in the long grass, and an old standing stone that Jimi believes is thousands of years old. 'Conversations always seem to happen around the standing stone. Someone once told me they were where communities used to gather.'

This is fitting, as much of Jimi's focus and energy in recent years has been building his own community at Hunting Brook, welcoming displaced people including asylum seekers and refugees to visit the garden and volunteer. Some have even gone on to train in horticulture. 'That feeling was always a little bit missing here, and it could be kind of lonely when the garden was closed and everyone would go. But now I feel that sense of community is building. And going out into the garden is so powerful. On our volunteering days, we changed it so the first thing we did was a walk in the woods. Everyone relaxed and started talking about plants in their own countries. I want to give them that safe place and a sanctuary they can come to.'

It has totally changed Jimi's outlook, giving him a new sense of purpose and diminishing his desire to get away in the off season. 'Like a lot of gardeners, I was always running away from winter, with that feeling of wanting to be in another place. I'm not running away now. I stayed home last winter and really enjoyed it, and I think it was that sense of community. I didn't need to be anywhere else.'

CORNERSTONES
DOGWISE JOHN FISHER
WILDING
Quiet Spaces
Mr & Mrs Smith Hotel
Home
RAIN GARDENS
Room Outside
BEACH CLUES
21st Century Hotel Graham Vickers
Patrick Caulfield Paintings

MARTHA KREMPEL

MANY GARDEN DESIGNERS speak of bringing the outside in, but there are few who would be as brave and bold in this as Martha Krempel. Sitting in her warm, welcoming kitchen, it's impossible to ignore the giant cactus-like euphorbia growing straight out of the floor.

Beyond, it is echoed in shape by a multi-stemmed river birch that grows in her small but striking courtyard garden. It's a stylish little backyard with an outdoor fireplace and spaces to dine and lounge, but also offers the perfect view from inside in every season through a full-height wall of Crittal windows. 'I wanted to be able to enjoy the garden in the rain,' she says. 'It was about having a space where you could feel like you're in the garden but you're not in the garden.' The profusion of houseplants all around further heightens this sense of lushness.

Martha is well versed in creating picture-perfect spaces. She is a Renaissance woman who has lived many overlapping creative lives: sculptor, gallerist, costume designer, fashion stylist, furniture fabricator, club promoter, studio manager and interior designer, to name but a few. She even once acted in a toothpaste commercial. All these roads, however, eventually led to what she considers her true calling in garden design.

She grew up in Yorkshire on the edge of the countryside, one of seven. Her parents, who had emigrated from Ireland in the 1960s, encouraged the kids to be outdoors and appreciate nature. They each had a patch of garden to look after, and Martha remembers a holiday job disbudding chrysanthemums at a nursery down the road. 'It was repetitive, but not as bad as working in the gooseberry bushes like my brother.'

Her mother educated Martha and her siblings on the great gardens of Britain and Ireland, exploring as many as possible. Her father was a doctor and a political medical cartoonist, who trained in art before studying medicine. 'He was a brilliant draughtsman, and was published in the national paper in Ireland regularly from the age of twelve. But my granny always said he had to go on to do a proper job, like medicine.' In contrast, Martha's mother was the one who suggested she pursue art as a career, and both parents instilled in her the belief that she could do anything she set her mind to.

During her fine art degree, she got into metalwork, learning laser-cutting and welding, and created large outdoor sculptures almost directly from her head. 'They'd ask me, "Where are all the drawings?" But I play around with things in 3D better than on the page.' After university, she moved to the capital and worked in a West London gallery. It was 1988, a time of dynamic cultural change, and she got to meet and mix with a vibrant network of established artists and thrusting young creatives.

Martha wanted to keep going with her metalwork sculptures on the side, but didn't want the responsibility and cost of her own studio. Ever resourceful, out of the blue she rang up the product designer Tom Dixon, known for making furniture and lighting, and offered to work 'as a minion' for him in exchange for use of his equipment. 'He thought I was really cheeky, but he said yes. I helped him goldleaf some of his famous S-Chairs, and he helped me make some of my sculptures.'

After a couple of years, she moved into men's clothing for TV and film, working for the costume designer Carlo Manzi, before heading to America, where she once styled the actress Jodie Foster for a shoot for German Vogue. Martha travelled around for a bit but, looking for her next move, contacted

college friend David Heathcock – an engineering wunderkind – to see if he wanted to do something together.

There was a recession in Britain and there were deals to be had, so many people Martha knew, or knew of, from her time at the gallery were starting up restaurants and bars, and she offered to make furniture and lighting for them. She was making ends meet running London club nights, including her own late club, which opened at 6 a.m. on Sunday mornings in a disused building in King's Cross. 'One night, someone came up and said, "I hear you're looking for studio space. There's a building in a goods yard across the road that's empty. Here's the key." It was perfect.' She and David built a forge and started their own furniture business.

One day they arrived to find a padlock on the door – they had been caught squatting by the building owners, P&O, who wanted a more formal arrangement, but let them stay on for a peppercorn rent. But between the damp and a few alarming encounters in what was then a notoriously dodgy area, they decided it was best to move to a new studio across town, where they could also do photo shoots. 'It's all about identifying a niche. I could see there was a gap in the market – nobody had done a decent studio in west London, and yet that's where most of the fashionistas lived then.'

It was around this time, in 1992, that Martha met her husband, Blair, at one of the clubs she was running. She credits Blair, who was then with ad agency Saatchi & Saatchi and is now an executive TV producer, with being instrumental in her success, a constant support and guide. 'I met Blair as he was starting his business and saw how he did it – he made it look easy.'

She shrugs off any suggestion that it was extraordinary how easily she moved between disciplines and wasn't afraid to jump into the unknown on a regular basis. 'In that period in the early 90s in London, it felt to me like anything was possible and

ABOVE Martha's small courtyard garden has a simple table and chairs at its centre surrounded by planting. **FACING TOP LEFT** The clever internal planting bed in her kitchen features a large euphorbia and a barrel cactus. **FACING TOP RIGHT** Martha also designed an intensive green roof to sit along the extension. **FACING BOTTOM** The outdoor fireplace creates a special atmosphere for family meals and entertaining guests.

'Anything was possible and people were really open … there wasn't any doubt in my mind we were going to be okay.'

people were really open to most things. It seemed like a natural, normal way to earn a living, and there wasn't any doubt in my mind we were going to be okay.'

So Martha and David took on the lease of a large warehouse, and Big Sky Studios was born – an ambitious, full-service, drive-in photographic studio. Soon, it was being frequented by the cream of the fashion and entertainment worlds. They were heady days. 'Prada would call and want to hang a cable car off the roof, and Dave would just say, "Sure, let me work out how to do that."'

When she and Blair got married and had a baby, however, she started to look at slowing down a bit. Designing interiors sets for the studio turned into actual work doing interior design in people's homes, which led to them asking her to design their gardens too. She did both for a while but realized that she really just wanted to do gardens. 'It was the tieback moment that did it,' she explains. 'One client couldn't decide between two different curtain tiebacks, and I thought, "I've got to stop this right now."'

Martha had continued to garden from a young age wherever she lived, even growing herbs in her student digs. Something about moving into garden design fully, seriously, felt right to her. 'I think I did all those other things on the way to doing this, because I didn't know this could be a job back then. Once I realized it could be a career, I homed in on it, and thought, yes, this is it. In garden design, I love the fact that you are responding to the site. You've got a brief to deliver, and then you've got your own artistic endeavour to marry that up with. For me, that's a beautiful mix.'

Seeking deeper knowledge and CAD skills, she went back to study at the London College of Garden Design in 2013. At the same time, she and Blair bought a new house in north-west London to take to pieces and rebuild. They designed it

LEFT The corridor that connects the kitchen to Martha's studio is fully glazed and contains a myriad of houseplants, bringing the garden into the house.

together, and she project managed the build at the same time as doing the course, which is famously intense and challenging. But there were benefits to trying to do both, as she got her first major garden design job from the architect who worked on the drawings for her house. After that, one job seemed to feed naturally into the next, and she has been busy ever since.

Garden designers usually hate being asked to characterize their style, protesting that every garden should be unique, but Martha has no problem drawing out her modus operandi. 'It's about colour, form and a balance between hard and soft landscaping. And there will always be trees with autumn and winter interest, fruit and roses.'

These are the backbone of her own garden too. Originally a hodgepodge space with lots of bamboo and a red-pillared Japanese pagoda, Martha designed the new concept for it alongside that for the house extension, turning the outdoor plot into an elegant courtyard of 9 × 6 metres (30 × 20 feet).

Now, a glazed corridor runs its whole length and links the main house to Martha's studio opposite. The garden is wrapped on three sides by the building, with a high brick wall enclosing the fourth side from the street. The clever cloistered feel is amplified by the sunken effect of the garden lying 60 centimetres (2 feet) below street level, in line with the house.

But trying to do something different is rarely appreciated by the planners, and she and Blair had a year-long battle with them to get permission for the extension – which left plenty of time for her to redraft the garden layout over and over again. 'I probably did thirty different ones. Because you can enter from four sides, it's really hard to design. It needs to look good from all angles, but also you can't block an entrance off, so you can only have the planting in certain areas.'

The final configuration and materials were inspired by a family holiday to America, where they spent time hiking in the desert. Looking down on the Colorado River in the Grand Canyon, Martha suddenly saw a way to make the courtyard work, with a pathway of poured concrete winding around planting and a patio of clay pavers. The colours she chose for the space were influenced by the coral tones of the nearby Painted Desert, and the whole space now glows peachy pink in the evening light.

With the garden in full view from every room, it has to look good 365 days a year. The evergreen climber false jasmine (*Trachelospermum jasminoides*) creates a green backdrop around the fireplace in winter, along with the blue-green leaves of *Melianthus major* under the peeling bark of the river birch. In early summer, the roses come into bloom, followed by a special moment in late summer when Japanese anemone 'September Charm' and miscanthus grass peak together. Then the quince above the low outdoor sofa fruits in autumn, when the acer in the far corner also begins to glow red.

Her enthusiasm for plants has spread not only through the house but also out on to the top of the extension, with an intensive green roof featuring sesleria grass and perennials such as salvias and rudbeckias, as well as flowering bulbs for spring – not for her the typical sedum roof mat. It shows that Martha is still taking risks and flexing those creative muscles in every way she can. 'It was important that it wasn't just a big patch, a grey roof. When you look down on it from the bedrooms, it's so pretty to see,' she says. 'The birds nip up there to collect nesting materials, and my neighbour says she feels like she should be paying me for the view. That's a result.'

FACING TOP A sofa bed and chair create a relaxing seating area in one corner outside Martha's studio. **FACING BOTTOM** Even though it is a small space Martha has planted trees, including an acer and a river birch, as well as roses and a honeybush.

JENNY BARNES

THERE ARE NOT MANY people whose name becomes a whole new word, but gardener Jenny 'Niff' Barnes gets her own verb. To those in the know in the world of gardening, to niff, or niffing, means to prune and train roses as she does into jaw-dropping sculptures of sweeping, twirling stems.

Some are great swirling curtains on walls, others are criss-crossing latticework shapes, and the most extraordinary are flowing free-standing forms. It's painstaking, often painful, work, clipping and manipulating evil thorn-encrusted branches in freezing, wet, windy conditions, but the results are astounding. 'It's more art than gardening, I think,' says Jenny. 'Between me and the rose, it's like a conversation. Or sometimes it's more of a fight.'

Although the practice does, as a side effect, help to create an abundant spread of flowers across the whole plant, it is ironic that her incredible artistry cannot be seen at all in the summer months, when leaves cover her sculptures, roses burst into bloom, and people are typically visiting gardens to see them. Instead, these intricate structures bring welcome interest just when it's needed most – the winter. They are a pleasure solely for those hardy enough to venture outside on the coldest days of the year.

Growing up on a farm, Jenny was never arty or particularly interested in plants. She was encouraged to be academic, so studied forensic science at university. 'But I hated it,' she says. 'I fell into a job working for National Grid as a gas trader. Lots of people would think I was lucky to have that job, but it was miserable. I was working in a high-rise office in Warwick with three thousand other people. I remember watching the maintenance people mow the lawn outside, wishing I could do that instead.'

This was to be a defining moment of clarity. She retrained in horticulture online, in the evenings, and started volunteering at Garden Organic in Ryton. 'With the qualifications and volunteering I'd done, it was enough to apply for apprenticeships, and I was offered one via the Professional Gardeners' Guild at Allington Castle in Kent.' She stayed there for eighteen months, before moving to Daylesford in Gloucestershire, where she worked her way up over three years to the role of senior ornamental gardener.

There was much excitement when the garden was featured in a book, *Secret Gardens of the Cotswolds*. 'We had a copy in the tearoom, and the picture on the front cover was of Asthall Manor. I thought, that's the garden I want to work in. I was completely blown away.' This Jacobean manor house in Oxfordshire was where the famous Mitford sisters grew up, and had a garden designed by Julian and Isabel Bannerman. It was just meant to be, Jenny says, as within a month her next-door neighbour told her about a gardening job going there.

Her interview went really well, or so she thought. 'I walked around with the owner and met Mark Edwards, the head gardener, and they were really positive.' But a phone call a few days later crushed her dream. 'They came straight out and said we can't offer you the job because you're a woman. It's a really physical job, and we don't think you're up to it.'

Jenny carried on as she was, but within a few weeks got another call. The person they had offered it to had not worked out, and she had her chance. 'But for that first year, it was absolute hell on earth because I had to prove myself. I went home for the first six months every single day and cried. I just didn't know if I could do it.'

Then, one day, Mark showed Jenny how to prune the wall-trained roses in a unique way he had developed. 'He is an artist. He went through it in about five minutes – he's a man of very few words – and then he let me get on with it, which was brave. I was on a ladder on the side of the house and he told me to come get him when I needed the ladder moved, and I thought, "No, I'm going to do it all myself." The next day he asked me to come and sit in the tool-shed with him for the first time, and I felt like I'd made it. Now, he's my biggest supporter.' She worked with Mark for three years and stepped up to become head gardener once he left. 'I carried on pruning and training the roses, and fell in love with them.'

Jenny went on to work as head gardener at Upton Wold in Gloucestershire and then Cottesbrooke Hall in Northamptonshire, a garden of rooms and English flower borders, where the owner was open to doing more with roses. 'It's all walls at Cottesbrooke, so there are loads of opportunities for big roses and climbers – I put in about a hundred roses in my first year.'

It was here that Jenny really got the chance to hone her own style, figuring out the best roses to use – large ramblers – and developing her process. 'I normally plant a rose, leave it for a couple of years or prune it traditionally to get some height, and then year three is a good time to start pruning like this.'

You can prune roses any time between October and March, but when you have a hundred to manage like Jenny, it's best to get going in September. She starts by first stripping all the leaves off the plant, 'so you get a really defined shape, which leads to a tight, clean structure. It's going to lose the leaves anyway, and most rose pests and diseases are borne on the leaves, so it helps to remove them.' A big rose takes about a day and a half to strip, and while Jenny is going along, she is also cutting out any dead stems, deadheading and pruning back the growing shoots.

'Then I step back and look at it, and start tying everything in. I need to be able to see the whole picture, and assess each stem individually. You can only do what the rose lets you do – it will tell you what it wants. If all the growth is going to the left, you have to make something to the left; you can't pull it to the right.' Rather like the Japanese principle of *ma* – the concept of an intentional gap or void – for Jenny the key to success in shaping the sculptures is in the negative space between the stems.

People are quite wary about crossing stems, but that's exactly what Jenny does, layering them one over the other and tying them tightly together with garden twine so they can't rub. She has a specific method of threading her spool of string

'Between me and the rose, it's like a conversation. Or sometimes it's more of a fight.'

FACING Rain, shine or frost, Jenny is out in the winter months wrangling rose stems into sculptural shapes. **ABOVE LEFT** Jenny's trusty secateurs are her only tool, and she usually doesn't wear gloves despite the thorny stems. **ABOVE RIGHT** Each stem is tied tight and neatly to the others with two-ply garden twine. **LEFT** Training large free-standing and wall-trained roses means Jenny often has to work from a ladder.

from her pocket and up under her collar, so it is always on hand and she doesn't waste any.

Aside from warm clothing and her trusty secateurs, she has no other fancy tools or kit, not even hand protection. 'I don't wear gloves because I want to feel what I'm doing, but I do tape the ends of my fingers, like a ballerina taping up her feet. It gives a little bit of protection against the thorns. Within a few days, my hands end up like leather. It's an occupational hazard.'

Encouraged by the response to her craft, in spring 2025 Jenny decided to go freelance to concentrate on roses, travel around and work in different gardens. She also hopes to create a new National Collection of rambling roses. She was approached about the idea by David Austin Roses while still at Cottesbrooke. 'The climate is changing, and roses are being discontinued because they are not coping with the conditions now. It's concerning that we're going to lose some of these roses if people don't look after them. So I started buying cultivars that are readily available, and got permission to take cuttings from other collections, and now have around 140 ramblers.' Building the collection would also give Jenny roses to prune, train and teach with, so people could one day use them for workshops and courses, and see the amazing things she can do with them.

'People are a bit scared of pruning,' says Jenny. 'I was when I started. You read the books, and it's so specific, and it's almost like if you don't do this perfectly, the rose will die. But it won't – you're not going to kill a rose from pruning or training. There is no wrong way of doing it. If I gave the same rose to ten different people and told them to create what they'd like, they would do ten different things. What's really nice about gardening is that everybody sees things differently. Mark used to love doing big target shapes with concentric circles, and he was great at leaving loose wands that would hang down. If I do that it looks like I've missed a bit. I have a perfectionist brain, so I prefer to prune everything tight, structured and rigid.'

Once people have seen Jenny's niffing, they always want to have a go themselves, but few have the patience to follow it through the way she does. 'They come on a course as they want

to be able to do it, but when they go home and have a try, they call me and say, "This is so mind-numbingly dull. Will you come and do it instead?" Because it's boring, it's cold and it hurts.'

Somehow, she doesn't mind these things – in fact, she seems to relish them. 'I like the fact that you can see what you've done. I'm not very good at jobs like bulb planting, when you can spend days working so hard, and then you've got nothing to show for it.

'One of the only things in the whole world that stops me overthinking is rose pruning, because I'm busy thinking about not getting stabbed or falling off my ladder. I get completely in the zone. I don't listen to music; I'm just by myself, sometimes with the birds, sometimes in the rain, stripping leaves off. I find that really therapeutic,' she says. 'It's sort of addictive. I don't want to stop. I will prune until it's dark.'

PREVIOUS Jenny taking a break having sculpted a huge ungainly rose in a wave shape over a stone wall in the Cotswolds garden of a client. **FACING TOP LEFT** A wall-trained rose in full bloom in summer after being worked on by Jenny. **FACING TOP RIGHT** Jenny checking in on her work at Cottesbrooke Hall garden, where she was head gardener for many years and still returns to help with rose training. **ABOVE** The herbaceous borders at Cottesbrooke, backed by a rose-spangled wall. Jenny planted one hundred roses while working here on the many walls of the garden.

JOSHUA SPARKES

SPEND THE DAY WITH Josh Sparkes, head gardener at Birch Farm, and by the end you're sure to feel like your brain is on a spin cycle. It's a constant, though pleasant, barrage of information delivered with captivating passion. You are in the presence of a true believer, you realize – and you're quickly considering joining the faith.

The new concepts and ideas come thick and fast, from syntropic growing and indigenous microorganisms to natural farming and polyculture, and you nod along, spellbound by his vision and tenacity. Because the proof is here to see. This patch of land in north Devon has been utterly transformed in the space of just five years from a silent dairy pasture to a beautiful, biodiverse and productive space.

For Josh, the key question is whether we can grow food in a way that also supports biodiversity. For most gardeners, the answer involves accepting previously unthinkable compromises. Weeds are welcomed here, and 'pests' of all kinds are left well alone. Everything has to be sustainable with minimal inputs, so he doesn't buy in any compost or woodchip. It also needs to be resilient, so he is trialling all sorts of perennial food plants that are better able to cope with climate extremes such as drought or flooding. There are no polytunnels here for growing undercover, and Josh neither nets nor fleeces his crops.

'I think of myself as a beetle farmer now,' he says, only half joking. 'What's different about how we grow at Birch Farm is that it is more about us humans being part of the landscape. You don't want to interrupt any habitat when possible, but instead use your growing to build habitat.'

Josh's big plan is establishing food forests. He has three examples at Birch Farm: one a 'romantic' edible forest garden for the curious home grower; a syntropic-inspired version that is focused on regenerating the soil in a self-sustaining system; and a third laid out for agricultural efficiency with easy maintenance and harvesting in mind. All of them share the same basic principle, however, of growing functional and productive plants in tiers or layers.

The top layer is typically 'system trees', for fixing nitrogen in the soil, and pioneer trees that grow fast and provide a quick crop such as fruit, nuts, timber or biomass for mulching. A shrub layer below might feature blackcurrants or sea buckthorn, while the herbaceous perennial layer usually contains culinary herbs. Sometimes there's a climbing layer with grapevines and a ground-cover layer with plants like alpine strawberries, and often there is a final root layer with Jerusalem artichokes or oca.

One thing growing this diversity of plants close together has proved to Josh is that rather than trying to outcompete each other for resources, they actually grow faster and are healthier when planted in communities. It is a lesson he has taken into the annual vegetable beds in the productive field here, where he grows in polycultures with herbs, roots, salads and more all in together, cheek by jowl.

There is a cut-flower garden alongside too, as well as a large pond, a small woodland garden and a rubble garden of flowers and grasses growing in the crushed up remains of an old power station. Josh also has a greenhouse he would love not to need but where, while they are establishing the farm and still growing annual crops, they propagate all their plants and create a homemade potting mix using the bokashi composting method.

It's all pretty experimental, so it's slightly shocking to discover that Josh does not come from an eco-warrior or permaculture background, but is actually a National Trust-trained, traditional, high-end ornamental horticulturist. He grew up in East Sussex surrounded by countryside. 'School wasn't my natural habitat. But I had the freedom to just basically run off and explore with my best friend. We'd build shelters, go on massive walks – it was a lovely childhood.'

He comes from a military family, so it wasn't a surprise when he joined the RAF on the cusp of eighteen. He served for five years, in places including Afghanistan, as infantry. 'You see real beauty and meet amazing people,' he explains, 'but you see horrible things as well – the destruction of war.'

He had to decide if he was going to continue his career in the military or do something else, so he left, not quite knowing what he wanted to do next. 'During those harder times in Afghanistan, I used to always retreat to that image I had of going through the meadows and the woods as a child with my friend, seeing all the wild flowers. I wanted to go back there, and a way that I thought I could do it was ecology. It was my grandmother who suggested retraining in horticulture.'

If he was worried about a repeat of his woeful school performance, he needn't have been, because studying plants, it turned out, was his thing. 'I actually became the top student in my year. If I'm interested in something, I'm hyper focused.'

This led to great opportunities, such as working at Sissinghurst for five years with head gardener Troy Scott-Smith just as the garden was going through a period of radical change. The famous White Garden became Josh's responsibility, and he went deep into researching how to improve the depleted soil there.

He also investigated meadows, taking a trip to Romania to work with farmers and find out about hand scything and making hayricks. And it was here, in a cabin looking out at the Carpathian Mountains, that he read the book that would change his entire trajectory: *The One Straw Revolution* by Masanobu Fukuoka. 'It was an awakening. It sowed the seed in my head of natural farming, and this idea of us co-existing and growing with biodiversity – a symbiotic relationship.'

So when he won a place on the National Trust's Triad scheme, a sort of exchange programme with Japanese and American heritage gardens, he was determined to use the experience to find out as much as he could. After working at several eminent gardens in America, including Longwood and Chanticleer in Pennsylvania, he went to Japan and was struck by the emotion-led approach of Japanese gardeners. It was as much or more about how a space made you feel than how it looked. 'We think about colour, form and texture, but they also ask: how does it move in the wind? What does the leaf look like in the rain? They think about all these deep messages, and it makes for astounding, impactful gardens.'

Fired up by what he was learning, Josh applied for and got a Churchill Fellowship grant to go back to America and get further insights into soil management and improvement methods such as composting, biochar and crimp rolling cover crops. He witnessed how they did large-scale food-waste recycling on the High Line in New York and how they brewed compost teas at Mt Cuba botanic garden in Delaware. He soaked it all up.

'I love that the American attitude is one of "let's try it." Everything is exciting, and it's all about trial and error. So it was difficult when I came back to the UK and worked in other gardens, and it was all "no, no, no: we've never done that before." It was crushing. When I asked why we were doing something, I was always met with "that's the way it's always been done," which I think is the most damaging phrase we have in our society.'

He soon got his chance to do things his own way when he became head gardener at Forde Abbey in Dorset. 'I cut my teeth doing massive tulip displays and reinvigorating the borders, taking my inspiration from places like Great Dixter and Packwood House. But then Covid hit, and all open gardens suffered.'

Josh realized that in public gardens that live and die by the mercy of ticket sales, it is difficult to implement radical ideas, such as leaving weeds to grow for habitat. 'So I wanted my next venture to be more of a food-growing project, where I could push the natural farming idea.'

He was inspired by another Japanese natural farmer called Yoshikazu Kawaguchi, who took the concepts from *The One Straw Revolution* and adapted them more practically into a market-garden setting. 'He realized that although these ideas are fantastic, when you run a business growing vegetables, you

FACING TOP Josh uses a broad fork to gently lift the soil for planting in the annual vegetable beds, helped by Twinkle the dog. **FACING BOTTOM** Growing in polycultures means different sorts of vegetables all grow together cheek by jowl with herbs, salad, fruit, shrubs and even weeds.

can't rely on just chucking things everywhere and letting it come up. The production of annual vegetables will always have this yin and yang effect. There is disruption, but you do it in the most minimal way.' Rather than digging over the soil to create beds, for example, Kawaguchi would sickle down the vegetation to plant vegetables, and put the cut weeds back on as mulch. This, thought Josh, was the sort of system he wanted to explore.

He must have manifested his heart's desire, because before long he was approached by The Collective, a linked group of small businesses based in the village of Woolfardisworthy. The founders, Michael and Xochi Birch, are American tech entrepreneurs best known for starting up the social networking site Bebo. Michael's family originally came from Woolsery, as the village is known, and he had spent time there growing up. When the local pub was in danger of being pulled down, some townspeople approached him to ask if he would consider saving it.

When Michael and Xochi pushed open the door, the legend goes, the menus were still sitting on the dusty tables and there was a tree growing through the roof. The Birches transformed it into a restaurant with rooms, and a bar the locals can call their own, and then went on to rescue the fish and chip shop and the village store as well.

To provide these three businesses with organic, sustainable food, the couple also took on land to make a farm and raise livestock. But they wanted a veg grower too. Josh pitched his big ideas around food forests and natural farming, and they went for it. He now had a completely blank canvas to test out his hypothesis. 'We had a grace period to try things, because we didn't know what any of it would really look like. That was the scary thing: this farm has always been like stepping into the dark. It was terrifying.'

Josh was right to be afraid. Converting these flat fields into a forward-thinking smallholding was a mammoth undertaking. In year two, which Josh has dubbed 'slug-pocalyse', there was

RIGHT The rubble garden features ornamental grasses and perennial flowers planted into the crushed remains of an old power station – a low nutrient substrate perfect for drought-tolerant plants such as blue eryngium and yellow rudbeckia. Piles of stones create habitat for invertebrates, small mammals and lizards. **OVERLEAF** In late summer the native wildflower meadow is filled with common knapweed.

'There's so much doom and gloom about biodiversity at the moment, and there's a call to arms for everyone who cares about nature to do whatever they can.'

FACING CLOCKWISE FROM TOP LEFT Nettles are harvested in spring for the kitchen at the pub; mashua is a type of nasturtium from South America which produces tasty salad leaves and tubers; sea buckthorn berries are packed with vitamin C; the leaves of toona, also known as the beef-and-onion tree, taste just like a packet of beef-flavoured crisps according to Josh. **ABOVE** The pond at Birch Farm is excellent for biodiversity and features edible plants including arrowroot, aquatic mint and fool's watercress.

an explosion of molluscs that decimated everything, even eating the leaves off the trees. 'One day, we picked two kilos of them off one veg bed – and we've got thirty-eight beds. The message of natural farming is always "observation over reaction", but when you have a mortgage to pay, it can feel ridiculous to do nothing.' They got through it because Josh is in the unique position of growing for chefs, who are happy to try unusual things on the pub menu and can adapt their cooking to whatever produce is available.

'And then, in the third year, it was like someone flicked a light switch, and the slugs were gone – well, they are still there, but they don't trouble us anymore. A big part of it is that the main slug predators – beetles, centipedes, frogs, toads, newts and birds – all started to slowly come back. Now our job is maintaining those habitats to make sure they have everything they need. We just had to hold our nerve.'

He and his team have managed to push through the harder times and make something that is a joy to be in. 'I've been lucky to be able to design the farm, apply these principles and try things. And now we will keep pushing it. Natural farming isn't a set of instructions – it's more of a philosophy, and you realize that it is a lifelong lesson,' he says.

'There's so much doom and gloom about biodiversity at the moment, and there's a call to arms for everyone who cares about nature to do whatever they can to make a difference. What's inspiring here is that we can see, with just a few changes, how quickly it can come back.'

FACING TOP The 'romantic' food forest shows how someone might create a layered, edible growing space with trees, shrubs, perennials, herbs and roots in a smallholding or garden. **FACING BOTTOM** The agricultural food forest is more regimented and aims to show how farmers can create healthy perennial food systems on a larger scale. **ABOVE** The polyculture rows are edged with a taller shrub row featuring plants such as willow as well as rough grass for slugs and beetles. **OVERLEAF** The rubble garden – in full bloom with golden rod – looks out over traditionally farmed fields that are a reminder of what Birch Farm once was.

KYLA LA GRANGE

IF THE SNAIL-SHAPED knocker on Kyla La Grange's door didn't tip you off that she's obsessed with gardening, then the hordes of houseplants in her living room would. The singer-turned-garden designer even has plants growing in her shower.

When she moved into her home in north London in 2019, it was not quite so green. Staring out the bifold doors into the shoebox-like 12 × 3 metre (39 × 10 foot) garden, all she could see was an enormous fig tree that blocked out the sun and a mass of grey concrete pavers. This might have put off most first-time buyers, but not Kyla. Having survived tough, topsy-turvy years in the music industry, the prospect of reworking this outdoor space didn't faze her – in fact, she says, she was itching to get started the day she and her partner, Dave, moved in.

And the transformation since then has been extraordinary, from that dark, hard-edged space into a kind of tropical fairytale. 'This is my little dream playground,' Kyla explains. 'I like anything that makes you feel you're stepping into another world, as if you've gone through a portal.'

A big inspiration is the garden Lotusland in California, created by another famous singer from the mid-twentieth century. Although Kyla's garden is miniscule in comparison, it does share a sense of wonder-fuelled eccentricity. 'It always needs to have a touch of the Brothers Grimm to feel magical for me.'

This sense of transportation from the real world was important for her music too, even when just starting out. 'I was the typical sad teenager who got given a guitar for their birthday,' she says. 'I loved writing songs in my bedroom, but never thought I could actually have a career in it.' All the same, once she left university with a not-so-useful degree in philosophy, she decided to give it a shot.

She got by working in bars and other minimum-wage jobs – 'it was grim,' she admits – and worked her way up from open mics to paid gigs and studio time, eventually landing deals with an indie and then a major label. Her sound, which she characterizes self-deprecatingly as 'gloom pop', ranged over three albums from angsty folk rock to melodic electronic songs. As well as producing her own music, a highlight of her career was performing with the dance group Faithless for two years on tour.

But it wasn't all as glamorous as it seemed. 'The music industry is notorious for giving people all sorts of issues, and I was no different. When you're on tour, you're travelling a lot and go from the adrenaline rush on stage to being on your own in a hotel room, crashing. If you're in any way inclined to anxiety or depression, it'll get you. I started to think, "I'm not cut out for this; I can't handle it." Gardening saved me.'

At the time, she was renting a small flat in Tottenham, north London, which had a tiny south-facing garden with no plants. 'I'd never lifted a finger in a garden before and didn't have a clue what to do, but when I would be home from touring, I started tinkering around. I had one episode where I started pulling up loads of paving slabs with my hands – I think my partner thought I was having a Britney-level meltdown – and digging out beds with just a hand trowel. Before I knew it, I was putting plants in.'

Hungry for knowledge, Kyla began reading everything she could about botanical names and took part-time courses in gardening. 'In the gaps from touring, it stopped me from having those lows, and worrying. In music, there's pressure on you all the time to be writing and coming up with the next single, but when I was gardening, I wasn't thinking about it.'

'The art of making a garden feels so much like writing a song. You start with nothing, and then you have this vision and it's all coming to you.'

She cringes now to think of what she planted and how. 'It was horrendous. I had such bad taste and made so many mistakes.' But watching the space transform felt amazing – so amazing that she decided to move out of music and into gardens, training to become a full-time garden designer.

And she has put everything she learned to use creating her own little haven: a fever dream of exotic-looking lovelies from different parts of the world including tree ferns, bananas and bamboo. Beneath these large set pieces are reams of colourful blooms, from red daylilies to the perennial pink sweet pea, and houseplants in pots that spend their summer holidays outside. It's a little symphony of a garden that, framed by the bifold doors, has to harmonize all year round.

Kyla chose smooth dark slate paving to help make the space feel bigger, but eschewed the usual patio right outside the door, instead putting a low planting bed directly in front of the glass, and making a 'catwalk' step to create a more engaging way into the space.

She has an eye for an interesting plant, from an unusual hardy schefflera to a black colocasia, and her favourite is a bigleaf magnolia that sits front and just off-centre in her raised bed. With huge leaves, around 75 centimetres (30 inches) long, and enormous flowers 'the size of your head', it's the one plant every visitor asks the name of.

Halfway down the garden, tucked almost out of sight behind verdant foliage, is a shabby chic arbour with built-in bench, smothered in climbers, where Kyla catches the morning light. 'Sit there having your coffee with the sun on your face and you can't be in a bad mood for long.'

Its once-painted-white metalwork is echoed at the end of the garden in a romantic 'twirly' arch with gates, which she spotted in a cafe-cum-junk shop in Kent. They mark the boundary, technically, but Kyla usually leaves them open so you can't see where the garden actually ends.

There is a little Neverland to be found beyond, as the garden backs on to an abandoned, now densely wooded, old railway track that is only accessible to residents – like their own private forest – giving a new meaning to the much-used designer phrase 'borrowing the landscape'. There were tree trunks and stumps piled around already, so Kyla began planting up a tiny section right outside her gate with ferns and woodland plants. There's also a small pond tucked away in the corner, and a swirly framed metal bench for reading.

As wonderful as her enchanting 'stolen' woodland niche is, the presence of all those trees does create some drawbacks. 'Even though it's a south-facing garden, because of the trees, it's quite shady. And thanks to all the leaves, the soil is crumbly and rich, which I thought was great, but it doesn't hold moisture for a second. Plants need to be quite drought resistant in this garden, so I've adapted by adding euphorbias and anemones – things that aren't going to need a lot of water.'

Keen to use every inch of space, Kyla also grows on the roof of her living room in pots, containers and tubs. 'It has become my place to practise planting combinations for clients' gardens, growing lots of grasses and perennials from seed to try together.'

Her transition from alt-pop star to 'hortist' may mean trading millions of YouTube views for quiet days in the garden, but she

ABOVE Pink perennial sweet peas and red daylilies offer pops of colour among the green in Kyla's small city garden. **FACING** Slate paving runs through the space, which she has filled with large-leaved exotics including tree ferns and banana plants.

was more than ready for this shift. 'As I got older and happier, I found I was writing less, and felt I was losing part of myself,' she explains. 'Then I discovered gardening, and it was that same buzz that was so familiar to me. The art of making a garden feels so much like writing a song. You start with nothing, and then you have this vision and it's all coming to you, picturing things in your head, but you're not thinking too much about the end result – it's a flow state.'

The heady rush of an audience's reaction is similar too, whether it's people sobbing along with your song or finding succour in your beautiful planting scheme. 'To elicit an emotional reaction to something you've made, just being able to make people feel something, whether that's with a song or a garden, it's such a special thing.'

But the main difference, and total relief, she says, is that with gardens, 'I didn't need to be sad to begin with, and channel this supercharged "emo" thing. I could actually be alright, and still get so engrossed and absorbed that I didn't notice the time passing. It's such a beautiful feeling. I'm never happier than when I'm making something.'

Kyla feels she has learned a lot in her transition from performing to plants. 'Once a song is finished, you usually know whether it's good or bad, but with a garden, there are so many variables that are uncontrollable. It gives you a more philosophical approach. That's been good for me in terms of learning to let go.' She has become more patient and better at taking losses through gardening, she says, because it teaches that you that there's nothing you can do. 'But then, you also have all these delightful things happen that you didn't expect. And that's even more joyful.'

TOP LEFT At the end of the main garden, a set of off-white gates opens on to a small woodland area with foxgloves and a tree fern. **TOP RIGHT** The seating arbour matches the style of the gates and creates a beautiful bower to sit under. **FACING** Kyla's sitting room is also filled with plants. The bifold doors open on to an unusual 'catwalk' step and a small planting bed.

RACHEL SIEGFRIED

'I NEVER GET bored of picking flowers, because every plant is slightly different,' says Rachel Siegfried. 'You get to know each individual plant, even in a row of seven hundred – when you look deeply at them, they all have their own little character.'

She started Green & Gorgeous, her flower farm and floral design studio in south Oxfordshire in 2007, and now looks after 2 hectares (5 acres) of organic flowers for cutting. Her main clients are brides – some who want the whole floristry shebang and others just looking for buckets of blooms for DIY weddings – but Rachel also opens the farm for pick-your-own-flowers days, sells fresh homegrown seed online and leads workshops on growing cut flowers.

The farm is a feast for all the senses in summer, with row after row of colourful blooms, many wonderfully fragrant. 'It's an oasis, a haven. You drink it up: the scents, the sounds. Since we've been here, because we grow organically, I've seen the bird and insect life increase.'

Rachel was always into crafts such as dressmaking and went to art college. 'I thought I wanted to be an artist, but it turned out that I wasn't very good at painting. I felt lost, and it was only when I started doing garden design that I rediscovered that side of myself and realized you can be an artist with plants.' She trained under designer-horticulturist Chris Beardshaw, and went on to create and maintain hospital gardens for the NHS for several years.

A six-month sabbatical travelling around South America fired up her interest in growing food, so she changed gears to work as an organic kitchen gardener in a beautiful walled garden on a private estate in the Cotswolds, producing veg, fruit and flowers over 0.8 hectares (2 acres). 'That's where the cut flowers came in,' she explains. 'I learned as I went along, growing lovely things for the big house. I enjoyed the veg, but the cut flowers really captured my imagination. It was the perfect marriage of ornamental and productive horticulture. I knew I'd finally found the thing that was right for me.'

She still clearly remembers cutting her first bunch of cut flowers. 'I loved how it encapsulated the garden in one handful, and seeing how the flowers worked together in the border, but also in the vase. I love that translation, and how you can then look at things closely when you have them in your home, and appreciate those plants in detail. Some people think that you are wasting them when you cut them for the house, but I see it as going deeper, getting to know the plant even more.'

While selling her vegetables at local farmers' markets, she noticed there were never any cut flowers. 'The slow food movement was taking off, but there was no slow flower movement. I had a strong conviction that it was something people would want.' So when her employers sold the estate suddenly and she saw an organic market garden up for rent, it was a no-brainer for her next move. 'The term flower farm didn't exist then, so I thought of it more as turning it into a cutting garden. Over the years, it got bigger and bigger, and became a flower farm.'

Rachel had never really had her own business before. 'It was quite a shock to have that safety net taken away and be at the mercy of the weather. I learned quickly that it's not a garden: it's farming. Scaling up is a huge thing, and continuity of flowers all season is tricky. I have to have all the elements of an arrangement – a focal element, a supporting element and a foliage element – ready to pick every week from April to October.'

When you do weddings, she says, you simply cannot have the dreaded focal flower gap. 'The hardest times are May and end of July or beginning of August – and these are obviously the most popular times to get married, so it can be challenging.' To avoid this, she plans at least a year ahead with brides, which helps her spot developing trends, like a white colour theme in late summer weddings, and then she orders, sows and plants what she needs to respond to that.

Her successional menu runs from early bulbs through to autumn seed heads. 'I couldn't live without anemones,' Rachel says. 'They are the first thing that flower for me in March, and get me started. Equally I don't know what I would do without the ranunculus that follow and all their colours.' She also grows tulips and Iceland poppies in spring, before the peonies arrive.

FACING TOP LEFT Green & Gorgeous has grown from a small concern to a large flower farm that requires transportation for getting harvested flowers back to base quickly. **FACING TOP RIGHT** Rachel arranges her homegrown blooms for weddings and makes them available in buckets for DIY brides too. **FACING BOTTOM** The farm has several polytunnels for annual flowers, as well as acres of perennial flowers such as sanguisorba and salvia. **ABOVE** Rachel checking the snapdragons and sweet peas in the polytunnel with her dogs Jesse and Romy.

'They give me such joy. I've got literally hundreds and spend a lot of time just standing out in that patch. They're like an old friend – you might have slightly forgotten about them, and then they come back and you remember why you like them so much.' Summer kicks off with masses of roses and rolls on through to a final focal-flower flourish from dahlias.

She grows most of her annual flowers undercover in her polytunnels, swapping out the bulbs for half-hardy annuals once they are over. Keeping the rain and wind off helps to produce the pristine-petalled blooms most brides demand. But Rachel is just as interested, if not more so, in growing perennials.

'It's more sustainable, not just for the land and the environment, but also practically for me as I've got older and the farm has increased in size. Perennials are more weather tolerant. With climate change, we've had some really tough years where annuals have completely failed. We can't grow sweet peas outside anymore, for example, so I've had to make the switch to keep the business going.'

She finds perennials, such as hellebores and thalictrums, more exciting creatively, too. 'It's the endless range. I'm always looking for new ones to try every year. They give you a longer

'That is the beauty of growing your own cut flowers. The possibilities are literally endless and I am always looking for new materials.'

cutting period than annuals because you can use them in different parts of their life cycles in so many different ways.'

Rachel also prizes shrubs, planting hedges and shelter belts across the farm for foliage and flowering and fruiting branches. She feels that she will be mostly growing these sort of permanent plants in the future, and she loves the range they give in her floristry work.

'I never make the same arrangement twice,' she says. 'That is the beauty of growing your own cut flowers. The possibilities are literally endless and I am always looking for new materials. Like any artist, I have a palette, and mine is a cultivated palette of plants. It's endlessly fascinating. I'm never bored, and I think I would be if I worked in a regular florist using imported stems. Some people find it restrictive to only use what's in season, but it makes you a better floral designer, because you have to use your imagination more. I get quite involved in it all.'

This extends all the way through Rachel's practice in a very holistic way, from sowing her own harvested seed and growing the flowers to arranging them and even making the right vessel to display them. 'Different seasonal flowers require different shapes of vases to show them off to their best, but I wasn't able to get the kind of vases I wanted. Why would I grow these flowers and then put them in something that everyone else is using?'

She took an evening pottery class and some courses, and then got her own wheel and kiln so she could start throwing vases and bowls that she felt reflected her style and personality, to make vessels that were the perfect fit with her floristry. Now, it's a real focus for her in the winter months, when she has more headspace to practise.

'It's quite meditative. You just get into the zone and don't think about anything else. It's pretty addictive actually, but can be incredibly frustrating. Just like with gardening, there is a lot of disappointment and unforeseeable things that go wrong, but you are driven to try again and keep going.' She has since created her own unique design of a footed bowl with a hollow base so that water and stems can go right to the bottom for better stability and appearance. 'For me, it's always been – with making my own clothes, growing my own veg, pottery – that I don't want to wait for someone else to do it for me,' she explains. 'It's a great feeling.'

Something else that makes her happy is opening the farm to visitors on summer weekends, with a 'flower bar' shop in the cool shed where Rachel does all her arranging with buckets of blooms lining every counter and most of the floor. She lets people go wherever they like and explore the whole garden.

'They disappear and come back smiling, calm. Many of them are regulars who come each week to have a little moment where they can be in the garden,' she says. 'It wasn't an intentional thing when I started, or ever part of my business plan, but to see people enjoying this is one of the best things about it. Otherwise, what's the point?'

ABOVE Rachel makes her own cut-flower vessels in her pottery studio during the winter. **FACING TOP** The perennial rows include scarlet and 'Coral Tempest' geums, stipa grass, lime-yellow *Euphorbia schillingii* and giant scabious. **FACING BOTTOM LEFT** Rachel also grows unusual plants such as these herbaceous clematis as cut flowers, using support cages. **FACING BOTTOM RIGHT** Pretty violas in caramel and burgundy tones from the Nature Antiques Shades series. Rachel has to have flowers in bloom every week from April to October. **OVERLEAF** The sunrise over the wider perennial beds which feature giant miscanthus, veronicastrum, eryngium, astrantias and eucalyptus.

JOHN LITTLE

IT'S HARD TO know where to begin with John Little. Maybe his green roof business, or his experiments using waste products as growing substrates and insect habitats. You could start with his penchant for using off-the-shelf materials to create beautiful, biodiversity-boosting garden features, or riff on the cause now closest to his heart and inked on his arm – care, not capital. There's just too much ground to cover, even when entertainingly delivered through his trademark fast-talking, irreverent, info-packed patter.

First-time visitors to Hilldrop, the Essex home he shares with his wife, Fiona Crummay, inevitably leave starry eyed with their horizons expanded and preconceptions blown apart, all fired up to start making their own compost heaps out of weldmesh, or perhaps dump a shopping trolley in their pond.

John is the renegade, Fiona the arch-facilitator, and Hilldrop is the *salon du jour* of the contemporary garden set. People from every facet of horticulture flock to this hub to learn about urban greening and brownfield gardening, and partake of Fiona's homemade cuisine, including her infamous vegan sausage rolls.

The plant-mad power couple met while volunteering at a local nature reserve, via a mutual friend. Fiona had moved from her hometown of Hull to do a postgrad and start her career in social care in London. Though initially unimpressed by her pal's attempts to set her up with John, she liked taking nips from his flask of whisky-laced coffee, and how comfortable she felt around him. Fiona decided to give him a shot, even offering to paint his house. 'All his neighbours thought he'd got off with the decorator,' she jokes.

Soon they were going on courses together, from hedge-laying days to reed-bed sewage workshops – not, perhaps, everyone's idea of high romance. For them, however, love blossomed through a shared interest in nature and wildlife. 'We both decided pretty early on: "This is the person I want to be with."'

So when an old, falling-down bungalow on a 1.6 hectare (4 acre) plot came on the market in 1990, they were determined to make it their home. They demolished what remained of the bungalow and replaced it with an experimental timber-framed home with a green roof – something they had both always wanted to try. 'Green roofs are very simple things,' says John. 'It's a case of making the structure strong enough, holding the soil on and letting the water off. If you do those three things, you can virtually do what you want.' Off the back of this experience, John started the Grass Roof Company in 1998.

Before this, he worked in the family business, a chain of shoe shops, but was always completely plant obsessed; as a child he once persuaded his grandfather to put a greenhouse in the centre of the lawn. When John's father decided to retire, the idea of taking on and continuing with the company did not appeal. Instead, they sold the shops, and John became a full-time gardener for a living. 'Turf in the back of a van, the whole thing,' he says.

Friends who were teachers suggested he get involved in designing outdoor spaces for schools, as at the time there was a boom in outdoor classrooms and school garden clubs, and this led on to work creating landscapes for urban social-housing developments. Often seen as 'green deserts', these in-between spaces are typically managed in an impersonal way by overstretched council-run teams or large servicing companies who pop in to mow and blow on a schedule.

John could see that no matter what new planting or facilities he designed and built for a space, it would only have limited, short-term impact without buy-in from the people who used it. So in 2002, when a maintenance contract came up for the grounds of Clapton Park in Hackney, east London, John seized the chance to do things a bit differently.

The development, comprising three housing estates of some 1,200 homes, is run by a Tenant Management Organization, meaning the people who live there decide how the place is looked after. It was only through this direct relationship with residents and the freedom it offered that John was able to foster a transformation through one simple act. He talked to them – or rather, he listened.

PREVIOUS John and Fiona's timber home features a green roof and looks out over a sloping site overflowering with sown meadow planting. **FACING, CLOCKWISE FROM TOP LEFT** The garden is a banquet for invertebrates with standing dead wood; cut down brush and garden clippings tied artfully to poles; gabion basket planters and perforated metal sand tubes; and gabion cob walls. **ABOVE** Fiona's side of the garden has curved raised beds filled with herbs and vegetables.

The multicultural population didn't want apple trees, low-maintenance shrubs and bare patches of mown grass, but vine leaves to make dolmades and space to sow herbs like coriander. Among other interventions over eighteen years, John delighted residents with the unexpected beauty of wildflower strips and rows of poppies on scrappy verges, and dug up lawns to create allotments where people could grow their own food. The project is now cited as a blueprint for how thoughtful stewardship in public landscapes can reduce anti-social activity and build community.

His latest crusade – care, not capital – has many echoes of this formative period, and is concerned with shifting investment away from infrastructure to those who actually look after parks, grounds and gardens. Success and innovation, he believes, is not down to always revamping places with flashy new designs, but valuing the skills of those who care for these spaces every day, and can connect face to face with the people who use them. 'Gardeners in public space cannot be playful,' says John. 'They don't have the money and the time to do that, and that's the problem.'

Playfulness is certainly something he and Fiona believe in at Hilldrop. When they bought the property, the gently sloping land was mainly laid to fields framed with barbed-wire fences. The couple put in some raised beds for vegetables, and set about planting hedges and trees and digging out the pond. Almost from the beginning, keen to reverse biodiversity loss, they created most of the planting via sown wildflower mixes.

Inspired by the local Canvey Wick Nature Reserve, an abandoned oil refinery, and the pits and quarries he loved to explore when he was young, John wanted to simulate brownfield site conditions in his garden. 'We're not doing anything new here. As a purely ecological space, there are better places, and there are definitely more beautiful and amazing gardens. We just combined the two.'

The focal points that stand out among the meadowy haze of flowers are not your typical urns, fountains and garden furniture. As well as brushwood-clothed telegraph poles and chic gabion baskets, there's John's old blue van sunk into a hollow, a 'veteranized' willow tree (where younger trees are deliberately damaged to create wildlife habitats found in old – veteran – trees), and a wall of waste rubble in a style John calls 'Essex drystone'.

His ultimate aim is to create biodiverse places that people like. 'We take a lot of care in the structural elements having an aesthetic to them.' There are sand-filled metal columns and planters, and sculptural standing deadwood, as well as cob blocks and artful log piles, in an effort to make wildlife-friendly features that also look good.

This is all inspiringly accessible, as John uses cheap, readily available construction materials in creative ways to design elements that are both functional and stylish. The solitary bees don't care if they nest in a cruddy old log or an attractively

ABOVE There is a sense of joy and fun in everything John and Fiona create, including the mannequin outside her greenhouse. **FACING** One of John's 'Essex drystone' walls made of rubble, beautifully built by craftsman Duncan Nuttall.

'Now we've got his and hers gardens. We like doing our own thing and it works most of the time. I enjoy my gardening more having my own space.'

drilled post, he explains, but if you want a nice garden, you probably will. Organizing materials neatly or giving them a frame or edge is the key: 'Otherwise it's just rubbish.'

Dotted around the garden there are also shipping container buildings and bicycle shelters with green roofs and habitat panels in a nod to the couple's daily bread. John recently moved his work operation to a yard on an industrial estate, but previously used home ground as his showroom and experiment site for green roof growing media.

He noticed that plants from the roof of one client kept seeding themselves into the driveway, creating exciting naturalistic effects and combinations, and he started to pay attention. Before long, he was trying out a range of interesting and unusual substrates on a larger scale in the garden, from broken-up old ceramics such as sinks and toilets to vast sweeps of sand excavated from nearby roadworks. These low-nutrient waste materials were perfect for growing wild flowers, unlike the garden's original heavy clay soil, and made for lower-maintenance plantings that needed a lot less watering and mollycoddling.

Not everything was an instant success, of course. 'There was that time you decided to do a river of crushed concrete from the house down to the road,' Fiona reminds him. 'Sixty tonnes of it. You can imagine what it looked like when it first went down. The poor postman just turned to me and said: "Your bloke's lost the plot, hasn't he?"'

Despite the naysayers, she has always been happy to support and believe in his vision – though she was once a bit taken aback at the arrival of a mountain of rather smelly calcium carbonate (also known as lime mud), a leftover from the sugar beet processing industry.

Fiona used to support him as undergardener too, but since the business has moved off site she has been able to claim a section in which to grow food and flowers as she wishes. She has taken ownership of a polytunnel and small greenhouse, and created a series of curved raised beds. Gourds hang from the trees and a half-dressed mannequin offers a quirky double take. 'Now we've got his and hers gardens. We like doing our own thing and it works most of the time,' she says. 'I enjoy my gardening more having my own space.'

John, for his part, has now gone all out on habitat creation. Meeting entomologist James McGill was a total game-changer, giving him and his gardener friend Benny Hawksbee a whole new focus in the garden. 'James said, "It doesn't matter how much bryony you've got – you won't get the bryony bee until you put a pile of sand somewhere, because they need that to nest." Once you've got that sort of information as a gardener, you can translate that into a landscape – and it actually only requires simple changes.'

As well as having a diversity of materials and embracing dead stuff – 'a big part of a functioning ecosystem' – this might include small things like digging a hole, creating a mound or leaving some bare bits. We all know about planting for pollinators, but invertebrates need places to live and breed as well as food plants. If you really want to increase biodiversity in your garden, you have to make it more complicated, like a brownfield site, with lots of different nooks, crannies and conditions.

A man of rare energy, John's social battery seems to charge up, not down, the more time he spends sharing his ideas or showing people around the garden. 'He's a hard man to take on holiday, and that's putting it mildly,' says Fiona. But they both get homesick so quickly it's ridiculous, he points out. And it's not like they ever need to go elsewhere. 'Everyone comes to us,' says John, 'and they are under the misconception that we're doing them a favour by having them here, as if it's a hardship. It's a joy, a luxury and an incredible privilege.'

PREVIOUS John's old blue Citroën van is sunk into the garden surrounded by hops, everlasting sweet pea and teasel, with a solitary bee tower standing sentinel. **FACING TOP** The pond outside the house offers another important habitat – everything John does now is about building biodiversity. **FACING BOTTOM** Log piles are an easy, nice looking and effective way of provided nooks, crannies and lying dead wood in a garden.

ROSANNA MORRIS

'IT'S NOT EXACTLY what I imagined for my life,' says Rosanna Morris. 'I didn't think I'd still be in the same streets where I grew up, but it's kind of beautiful in a way.' The artist and mother-of-three specializes in handmade botanical block prints with a unique style that is all her own – a contemporary twist on old wood engravings.

Her airy studio on the outskirts of Bristol city centre is lined with her evocative prints. They reflect a focus on the land – harvest, nature, abundance and a sense of simple, wholesome generosity and kindness. There's a latent optimism inherent in her work that puts you back in touch with the best version of the world and the people in it. It says: look at the bounty we can create, see how lucky we are.

'My art has always been about food, and plants, and growing, because of the food scarcity in my childhood. It's a bit of an obsession,' she explains. 'I come from a working-class family and grew up on a council estate on the edge of Bristol with a single mum. When we were really little, she put herself through university to study computer programming, and we had to live on her student loan, which was less than benefits. We were really poor, and I remember always feeling concerned about food.' When her mother got a job, they were eventually able to buy a house. 'It was in a rough area, but it was the only place we could afford.'

She lived just around the corner from where we now sit, and she remembers coming to visit the open studios once a year to see the artists working. 'I was so inspired to see that it was possible to be a full-time artist. There is a wonderful kind of synchronicity with the fact that I'm still here, working in this same building.'

But it wasn't a straight road from then to now. 'I try to explain to people when they ask me when or how I decided to be an artist that, really, I have never done anything else. There was no choice. It was the only way.

'I'm dyslexic and struggled growing up. I was slow to read and write, but I always drew. It was my way of communicating with the world, because I didn't feel able to do it with words. I communicated with pictures.'

At her school, they were dealing with big social issues, so Rosanna's falling behind slipped under the radar. But some tutors in the art department noticed her dedication and commitment, and organized for her to do extra GCSEs early. 'I didn't really go to my other lessons and I didn't get maths, English or science – I just did every possible art and design subject.'

This led to an art foundation course at Bristol School of Art, where she found printmaking. To give herself the artist equivalent of a 'trade', she went on to study illustration at Camberwell College of Arts in London, and travelled around Asia and Mexico, meeting her partner, Konstantinos, along the way. 'Quickly, we were having our first baby, without planning it, and moved back to Bristol.

'I kept saying I would get a part-time job in a bar or something, but he told me I had to focus on my art. His determination inspired me, so I kept going, carving prints at the kitchen table on wood that I found in skips, and hand-printing with a wooden spoon. I had my baby next to me, crawling on the floor, and fitted work into nap times and bedtime, or got up early in the morning and worked before he woke up.'

She put on some mini exhibitions and gained commissions for projects like album covers for folk musicians. One of

her big breaks was being asked to create a calendar for the Land Workers' Alliance, whose aim is to improve the lives of people working the land in the UK. The studio followed, and provided a venue for teaching courses, and Rosanna has never looked back.

'But in my biggest dreams', she admits, 'I wanted my own land and space to be in nature. I think that's what's behind a lot of my art. The times when I've made the best work have been when I've actually not had nature at my fingertips. My most popular prints come from this point of sadness and longing, and creating something hopeful to make myself feel better.'

Rosanna does have a garden at home now, with a little greenhouse, but it is quite small and wild, she says. So it was exciting when she managed to get an allotment around the time she had her firstborn. 'I didn't go to baby groups or play sessions. We would just go to the allotment. Even now, I don't have any other hobbies. I like to grow and it makes me feel happy. I need to have my hands in the soil to ground myself.'

She practises 'no-dig' gardening 'because it's just easier', and grows 'insane' amounts of cucumbers, as well as raspberries, potatoes, pumpkins and beans, especially 'Gigantes', a big fat butter bean from Konstantinos's home region in northern Greece.

'I love beans because life is busy, and sometimes you don't get to harvest them on time, but they will dry and you can keep them for winter. So, you don't miss some perfect moment where you have to eat them, which suits us, because life is chaotic with three children.'

Recently Rosanna has been growing more flowers, both because they bring so much joy and to dye her special natural papers, which are handmade in Nepal from coppiced shrubs: a renewable, sustainable resource. 'The papers are all sun dried, and they look really raw, with all sorts of random shapes and funny things in them sometimes.' She also makes a lot of her

FACING TOP Rosanna grows vegetables, fruit and flowers on her allotment. **FACING BOTTOM LEFT** She often comes here to work, inspired by plants and nature, drawing what's in front of her or what has been percolating through her mind. **FACING BOTTOM RIGHT** Rosanna's practice and growing is part of and not separate from her family life. **ABOVE** Shelling beans with her youngest son on the allotment, under a homemade arch hung with squash and cucumbers.

THE REVOLUTI
IS
FERTILE

own inks from natural pigments she finds, such as yellow ochre from the clay under an old pond on her allotment and a red pigment from an old wall nearby.

For a new piece of work, her process starts with pencil or ink drawings in a sketchbook. 'Usually, it is something that keeps repeating in my mind, that I can't shake and keep visualizing again and again.' She draws it on to wood or lino – often reclaimed and salvaged pieces of merchant ply or old flooring, which she finds at a scrap store or is gifted by friends who are renovating houses.

She uses first pencil and then permanent marker to make the design feel bold. Once the marking up is done, she starts to carve with tiny gouges, removing all of the white space. 'It's the opposite of drawing, where you're making a mark. With lino, you're taking away everything you don't want to make a mark, flipping it on its head. By the end, it is a giant stamp, which I cover evenly with ink using a roller, and then pass through my press.'

Rosanna has two presses, one of which was custom built in the studio by Konstantinos, and christened Bouboulina. 'She is named after a Greek naval heroine who led an army of ships against the Ottoman Empire – a single mother with five kids, a powerful beast of a woman. The press is massively over-engineered – it's one of the biggest ones in the UK and will be impossible to ever move out of here.'

Food sovereignty and self-sufficiency are still at the heart of her work, but like the Mexican printmakers she so admired on her travels, her prints also deal with wider social and environmental causes, from diversity and injustice to community and motherhood.

Sometimes the messaging is implicit and wrapped up in her captivating imagery, and other times it is more explicit, but hers is a gentle revolution. 'I do consider myself an activist in my heart. How could you not want to change a system that isn't fair for the majority of people? I just do it quietly, with flowers.

'I feel really privileged to be able to do this job that I love so much, and raise my kids,' she says. 'I'm my own boss, and it means that if I want I can just go to the allotment and draw all day.

'It's not a lifestyle that you choose if you want to be wealthy, but we are rich in choice and time.'

'It's not a lifestyle that you choose if you want to be wealthy, but we are rich in choice and time.'

FACING, CLOCKWISE FROM TOP LEFT Rosanna's studio, where her prints on handmade paper decorate the walls; she works on lino, first drawing out her idea before scoring out the silhouette; it is painstaking work removing everything you don't want to make a mark; she rolls ink on to a finished linocut block before placing it in the press and rolling a heavy drum over it. **ABOVE** A finished linocut print coming off the press.

and grow some grass for the dogs to play on, and that failed quite miserably.'

With the lawn idea out, he instead expanded the beds, leaving a small pathway through the centre, and laid a patio with bricks reclaimed from a house renovation around the corner. 'There was no predetermined plan. It wasn't all planted at the same time or designed with this in mind – it's been an evolution.'

The shady side features a fern garden and the sunny section has more of an English cottage-style feel, with the escapees from indoors giving an enjoyably off-kilter, mash-up vibe around the seating area. 'Fusing all these things together rather unconventionally might jar for some people, but it's an exciting playground for us,' explains Steph.

This idea of experimenting and not conforming to the typical is core to Steph's work. Always gifted, she got an art scholarship at the age of eleven and it was obvious that she would go on to art college. 'It was always going to be painting; it was something organic that came out of me without really trying. It was just a thing that I did.'

She moved to Liverpool with her then-partner, where she painted for a living and sold vintage clothing as a side hustle for a few years. It sounds like the idyllic bohemian dream, but Steph admits that she suffered from extreme anxiety for a number of years. When her relationship ended and her father got ill and died quite quickly, she came back to London to forge a new path for herself. 'I tried to grab hold of something; anything to latch on to as a reasonable career. Photography almost happened as a default.'

She has spent the past decade building an impressive portfolio of portraiture, shooting for fashion houses like Gucci and Versace, brands such as Nike and Mugler, and magazines including *Vogue Italia* and *Dazed*. Captured on medium-format film, her pictures often have a dreamy quality, even as they challenge or surprise you with hidden layers of subversive meaning and humour. They make you want to keep looking.

'My work is centred around the body – particularly women's bodies – and undermining or at least counteracting a lot of enforced stereotypes around that.' A career highlight was winning the 2024 Taylor Wessing Prize – one of the world's

FACING, CLOCKWISE FROM TOP LEFT The couple's main room is completely clothed in houseplants, reaching up to and hanging from the high ceiling; in summer many of the more tender plants are given a holiday in the garden among more typical herbaceous perennials; cacti and succulents including coral cactus, aeoniums and golden rats tail cactus edge the seating area in a collection of ceramic pots; Tom filled the garden with plants when he moved in. **ABOVE** The garden has one sunny side and one shady side divided by a brick path. The sunny side features heleniums, alliums, geums and knautia.

'I make sculpture for the space, and it could be kinetic, abstract, figurative or wildlife. I love that exploration.'

'I'd always thought there was some strange alchemy in it. But then I gave it a go and it was transformative. I loved it, more so than painting.' He added a few sculptures to his exhibit for the fair circuit, and they sold out. 'We realized it was a winner – and it just progressed from there.'

Although he started with clay, Simon couldn't get the finish he wanted, so tried various other materials, including epoxy resin typically used for car body repairs, 'because you can actually shape it, carve it and smooth it down so you get lovely forms.' Monique wouldn't recommend it. 'The smell! I think it slightly rotted his brain,' she says.

PREVIOUS *Disappearing Worlds* is one of Simon's newer kinetic-style works. **ABOVE** Simon welding in his studio at the garden. **FACING TOP** *Leaf Spirit*, a bronze by Simon, seen across the lake. **FACING BOTTOM** Monique and Simon also showcase the work of other sculptors at the park. Here, *Icarus Rising* by Nicola Godden makes an impression beside a sphere by Charles Elliott.

His practice developed from small early pieces, mostly of wildlife, to making models or maquettes that were then used to cast pieces in bronze in a foundry. Simon always creates directly with the material without plans or drawings, refining the forms over several versions if necessary.

The gallery that represents him in London started to get requests for these larger works, the most popular of which is *Isis*, a large, elegant bird sculpture. It has since found a home at both the National Museum of Wildlife in the US and Hyde Park in London. Another well-known piece, which he exhibited at the Chelsea Flower Show, is *Search for Enlightenment*, with upturned heads looking skyward – inspired by a night stargazing with friends in South Africa.

Things were going so well that, having rented for years, Monique and Simon decided the time was right to buy somewhere. They started searching online for their wishlist: a house with a couple of acres and a barn for a studio, all within budget. 'The first thing that came up was this place, which was 26 acres, loads of buildings, and double our budget,' says Monique. 'There was no way we could afford it.' At the time, however, it was a working fishery for anglers, doing good numbers, and this tipped the balance in terms of being able to get a bigger mortgage.

They moved in during the bleak days of January 2007, but their spirits were high. As well as all their stuff, Monique brought hundreds of plants in hessian bags, dug up from her previous garden, to start planting the spaces around the house; Simon brought some of his large sculptures out of storage to put around the lakes.

The pieces looked so good in this natural, wide-open setting that he made some more, and they began to plant up areas to act like frames for these works, so clients could come and see the pieces in context. 'Every time we put a sculpture in, we improved an area, and then naturally we had to maintain that area,' says Monique. 'Our staffing costs started to go up.'

The couple decided to try opening the garden to the public, to help it pay for itself, starting with a trial run of two weeks. They didn't know what to expect, but they needn't

have worried. 'The atmosphere of the whole place changed,' explains Monique. 'It was extraordinary. The energy was quite remarkable.' The open garden proved so popular that after three days they told the fishermen they wouldn't be opening the fishery again, and the carp are now enjoying a well-earned retirement.

Things have continued to evolve since then, with the development of a bistro-style cafe, as well as a store selling crafts by local artists and makers, an artisan food shop and a gallery. There are events such as a well-being festival and bring-your-dog days, and several cabins, pods and spaces for people to rent for the day for a celebration or picnic. The garden has even done a stint on TV as the setting for *Your Garden Made Perfect*.

Monique's main challenge with the garden is the extremely free-draining soil. 'It's hard to believe when we're surrounded by so much water, but our water table is really low.' This has been exacerbated by climate change, with erratic weather patterns making it difficult to establish and nurture woody plants from all over the world. She also has issues with naughty squirrels and rampaging deer chomping on her roses and bamboo, but takes a fairly lax approach, as she understands the importance of biodiversity in all its forms to an ecosystem like a garden.

'When we came here, the place was a bit of a desert for wildlife, because it was all mown grass,' she explains. 'We stopped mowing and suddenly we had more insects, more birds. We planted trees, put in dead hedges and made log piles. Now we have more than 140 species of birds, and have been declared a site of nature conservation interest by the Dorset Wildlife Trust for our dragonflies and damselflies. We think of ourselves as nature guardians.'

TOP LEFT Monique checking on the kitchen garden which features a host of edibles and flowers. **TOP RIGHT** Everywhere you look there are artistic details such as these stone threaded ropes hanging from an apple tree. **FACING** The striking *Search for Enlightenment* by Simon was inspired by a night stargazing in South Africa.

Her passion for conservation extends to caring for what one might call the strays of the plant world. She has created a National Collection of the much-maligned yellow-flowering shrub forsythia – 'not everyone's favourite,' she admits – and is presently collecting and propagating rare and critically endangered conifers such as glyptostrobus and sequoia.

'When you say "conifer", most people think, "Oh, those things from the 1970s that nobody wants." But they are incredibly ancient and important – they're the most threatened group of plants on the planet. I always tend to seek out the underdogs, the ones that need some love and attention.' She became enamoured with these plants while volunteering at the nursery at Royal Botanic Gardens, Kew, for several years, and has since tracked down and rescued about sixty-four out of around eighty-three different RHS-recognized threatened cultivars and species.

One of Monique's proudest moments was when Sculpture by the Lakes became an accredited botanic garden – one of only fourteen in the UK. 'It was a fantastic accolade and it opened a lot of doors, because it means that I can contact anyone in the network about plants on their list. It doesn't matter whether you're small like us or a big, posh botanic garden like Kew or Edinburgh – all gardeners love to share.'

Simon also revels in the opportunities the garden has given him and how this has influenced his work. The diverse styles on display include large bronze statues, huge wind chimes, swing seats, newer kinetic works, engraved stone globes and Corten-steel words. 'One of the joys of having your own sculpture park is that, as a sculptor, you don't have to stick to a genre,' he says. 'I make sculpture for the space, and it could be kinetic, abstract, figurative or wildlife. I love that exploration.'

Monique and Simon also exhibit pieces by other sculptors and artists throughout the park, choosing works that satisfy their core criteria of beauty, skill and emotion. 'To be a successful piece of art,' says Simon, 'it has got to have all three.' Spend a few hours wandering the peaceful paths of this intriguing garden, and you're sure to agree.

PREVIOUS The Wise Walk draws the eye down a snaking row of cloud-clipped evergreen lonicera to the sculpture *Barn Owl III* by Carl Longworth. **ABOVE** *Serenity* by Simon seen through the wisteria tunnel, which also offers a frame for roses and clematis. **FACING** The Wise Walk has a spine of fountain grass and is lined with a colourful border of perennials including salvias and rose campion.

ALICE VINCENT

'I THINK IF YOU told sixteen-year-old Alice, "You're going to be a writer," she'd have been a bit disappointed,' says Alice Vincent. As a teenager, she was all about the visual arts – painting in oils, mixed media, sketchbooking – but when it came to choosing a university course, she took a different track. 'I chose English literature, I think out of cowardice. It seemed easier to live a life with words than pictures.'

Her younger self might be dismayed at where she has landed, but chickening out back then has led to an enviable, glittery-looking career – the sort I'd like to have when I grow up. It stretches across music and the arts to gardening and the female experience, and mixes new and legacy media roles from podcasts and a newsletter to books, newspaper columns and features in magazines like *Harper's Bazaar*.

Somewhere in there – between interning at a youth fashion magazine in New York, working as a music journalist for the *Telegraph* and becoming an author and commentator – Alice found plants. Young and hip horticulture enthusiasts are like gold dust, and her early adventures in gardening inspired a millennial milieu who were keen get their hands dirty. Though she would doubtless rail against the label of a cool kid, I've always thought of her as the Alexa Chung of gardening – how many other garden writers have had their wedding featured in *Vogue*? – but her dual citizenship of these different worlds hasn't always been straightforward.

'When I was a music journalist I had to hide my gardening affinity,' she says, 'and then once I became better known for gardening, people were always shocked to find out that I used to be a music journalist. There's no reason why a certain type of person should or shouldn't garden. People just like to put you in boxes, and gardening occupies a very specific box. It's felt that gardening is this polite hobby that the elderly partake in, and people don't realize that it's quite filthy and sexy and generative. The garden is an endlessly creative source.'

Her initial steps in gardening, documented in her book *Rootbound: Rewilding a Life*, were via pots on a balcony. Several years later, she moved with her dramaturg husband to a ground-floor flat in Brixton, where she could get stuck into her first real garden.

It had 'the world's biggest patio,' she jokes, 'with really hideous stepping-stone paving slabs'. Existing planting included a lot of ivy, a ratty bit of grass, a decrepit plum tree (which they felled) and a large choisya bush (which Alice crown raised). She dug out a long bed and filled it with flowers, arranged her many pots on the sunken path by the back door, and just enjoyed herself.

Looking back now, Alice can see that in those early years the garden had a sense of delight, freedom and easy beauty – it's a bit like, she says, looking at a photo of your younger self and thinking how lovely you were back then, but you didn't, couldn't, realize it. It was a place to hold carefree, fizz-swigging parties with friends and try out growing in the ground for the first time.

Indeed, the possibilities of this small rectangle of soil went to her head for a bit. 'At first, I would see any nice thing on Instagram, buy the plant and put it in,' she explains. 'It was absolutely insane, but also joyful. A mad, cottagey, completely hodgepodge, jack-in-the-box garden. It wasn't remotely sustainable in time, effort, energy or luck.'

Determined to put more shape on the space, she invited Susanna Grant, a gardener-designer, to cast her eye over the colour scheme and offer some direction and guidance. Susanna quickly identified a thread of pale pink flowers with white

'There is beauty to be found in however people make their gardens, because they're so often a demonstration of what is important to them.'

and muted yellow accents – a theme Alice had hitherto been unaware of – which, if embraced, could result in a pleasingly cohesive planting. Alice likens the exercise to having a personal stylist, but for the garden. 'It was like her looking at my wardrobe and saying, "Well, you never wear that, and you always wear this, so just go with it."'

Big changes were planned, however, to accommodate the transition to family life. Alice's small office in the flat was to become the baby's nursery, and so the hunt began to find a suitable, affordable garden office. They settled on working with contractors to upgrade a stylish shed model with insulation and power, and looked at what else they could do while the builders were on site, such as lifting the patio and reusing all the old slabs.

Building work is challenging at the best of times, but was particularly so in this case as Alice had only just given birth. 'I was three weeks postpartum. I just sort of stood there delirious, offering cups of tea I never made, with the baby strapped to me, vaguely shouting instructions. Watching the garden be destroyed, and thinking, "What is happening in my life?"'

Alice's writing hut went in, as did a new cherry tree in the middle of an expanded lawn, and the whole timbre of the space changed. The first thing you see as you come out into the garden is that tree, *Prunus* 'Accolade', which puts on a beautiful show of blossom in spring and is in full glorious view out the back windows of the house.

Beyond is the writing hut, a small and cosy 2 × 3 metres (7 × 10 feet), painted black to match the dark, receding boundary fences. 'It's a liminal space between my responsibilities of the house and the garden – almost another world in itself. I love writing outside of the house; it's such a luxury. I like sealing myself off from "the pram in the hall", and I feel so lucky to have a space that, by its very nature, means I have to inspect the garden every day before I even get to my desk.'

This separation of church and state is important for her process, but Alice is not precious about her writing practice. 'I know some people banish their spouses from the house and need to write at certain times with a certain pair of socks on. Inside my working space, it needs to be calm and, crucially, silent. But beyond that, I tend to just increasingly know and trust that I'll turn up, open the page and something will come out,' she says.

'I write my books on the Tube, and on the way to nursery pick-up. I do a lot of writing in my head and by hand, plotting and note taking, planning out on big pieces of paper. I'm quite patient with myself in knowing that I have to think for quite a long time before I write anything. But I only have so much childcare, so I treat it like a job and have hours I keep.'

Inside the hut, one set of windows looks back to the house, the lower wall of which Alice has painted a striking shade of muddy, plaster pink. From here she can take in her beloved pots and a new border, as well as the lawn, which she leaves to grow long all summer. Out the other window, thriving somehow between the hut and the fence, is the crown-raised choisya, which offers evergreen interest all year and opens its white, scented blooms first in spring and then a second flush, just when you really need it, in autumn.

The most recent developments in the garden are in the opposite corner, where the original long flower bed has been replaced with a mini gravel garden and seating area, including a black-painted arbour with bench. As well as being guided by the area's sunny, hot, dry character, Alice put the seating just a few steps from the door of her hut, so she can walk directly out there when the weather is nice. 'The two are in symbiosis,' she says.

'Writing now feels like a really literal direct expression for me, because I write quite a lot about my life, and I increasingly go to the page to figure things out. But if I'm stuck with knowing what to write, gardening usually unlocks it.'

Over the past few years, through projects including the *Why Women Grow* book and podcast, she has been preoccupied with the question of why she herself is drawn to working the

FACING TOP LEFT Alice painted her outside wall an eye-catching shade from Lick called Red 03. **FACING TOP RIGHT** Outside Alice's black-painted garden office, she grows plants such as diascia and miscanthus in dolly tubs. **FACING BOTTOM** She painted her arbour seat the same black as the office and the fence, and used it as a frame for climbing roses and a potted pelargonium.

soil. 'I think it's an outlet for my creativity in the same way that art used to be. And while I do miss having an art practice, gardening allows me that. I get into this sort of strange flow state when gardening, where even though I am a planner, I do not need a plan. I just like to be out there and see where each decision takes me.'

The quandary of becoming known as a garden writer, however, is that there is an expectation of what your own garden is and looks like. 'I've had to learn how to trust myself with what I want to do out there,' she says, gesturing to the garden, 'and a lot of that is by shutting off the noise of what other people are doing in their gardens or what I should be doing. That's hard, because the horticultural establishment is quite a lumbering beast. It's difficult to go against it.'

With refreshing frankness, she reveals how there was a time when, in anticipation of me arriving to interview her, she would have rushed out to buy lots of new plants and do lots of tidying and pruning to make the garden look amazing for my visit. 'Instead, now I'm like: this is what it looks like. Do what you want with it. We put so many expectations on ourselves, of beauty standards, of how we should behave, of what space we should occupy and what those spaces should look like. I want that to be part of the messaging: that you don't have to be out there pruning your wisteria on the dot of every season.

'And it has felt so freeing to just say, fuck it, let it go and see what happens. I'm at this point in my life, with a young family, trying to navigate a new working life and motherhood on my own terms. It's nice to have this area of rebellion where I don't have to do anything but observe.'

Anyway, she says, everyone's garden is beautiful if you have the right outlook. 'There is beauty to be found in however people make their gardens, because they're so often a demonstration of what is important to them. I like gardens that people have done their living in. If I don't feel comfortable enough to roll around on the grass, it's probably not where I want to be. To be a "proper gardener", you just need an appreciation of the world that we share with other living things.'

FACING By the steps up to the garden by the back door, there is a collection of eclectic containers, including chimney pots, old wash tubs and window boxes filled with everything from an acer to heuchera, ferns, fatsia and ivy. **ABOVE** Feather reed grass rubs shoulders with the foliage of euphorbia and gladioli.

DIG FOR
VICTORY

DEAN CHARLTON

DEAN CHARLTON likes old things – he is what you might call a young fogey. Visit Hooton's Walled Nursery in Rotherham, and you will find this in evidence everywhere, from the stylish 'drystone skip' walls he has constructed from recycled bottles and old bricks to the loud 'brring-brring' of his ancient rotary telephone echoing through the greenhouses. 'It just takes you back,' he says wistfully. 'And when you pick it up, there's even an old crackle on the line.'

His nostalgia for the old days and old ways extends beyond novelty or aesthetics (though he does have a penchant for a good pair of trouser braces). 'Take tools – there are so many terrible plastic tools you can buy now, and they snap, so you go and buy another one. Before, tools were built for gardeners, even customized. I always say choosing a garden fork is like Harry Potter with the wand – you need to find the right one.'

It's a line of thinking that's stood him in good stead as he and his father, Glenn, took over the neglected site at Hooton's in 2023. Originally the walled kitchen garden of the big house across the road – part of the Wentworth estate, established in the 1700s – had been a nursery for decades selling bedding plants and hanging baskets.

Although it was a long time since it lived its best life, Dean could see the bones of something great. The key infrastructure was still somewhat there, with several derelict greenhouses, frames for polytunnels and a scrappy collection of sheds, which all leaned so precipitously that a misguided sneeze might send them the way of the little pig's house. But there were water valves and a kinked-up irrigation system, capillary heat mats for keeping plants frost-free over winter, and a row of three 200-year-old espalier pear trees that Dean just knew would bring the character he was looking for.

As any grower will tell you, the biggest challenge in starting a nursery these days is finding the land. Dean had been on the lookout for a few years and jumped at this opportunity, racing up from Great Dixter Nursery in Sussex, where he was working, to pitch his vision for the site to the new estate manager. A whirlwind six weeks later, the deal was done, and Dean was back in his hometown with a proverbial mountain to climb.

And yet, knowing his origin story, it's hard to imagine he would have ended up doing anything else. He recounts entrepreneurial exploits from childhood like saving discarded seedlings from his dad's thinnings, and repotting them secretly to sell at the end of the drive with his little sister, Lauren. He chuckles at the memory. 'We'd sit there for hours and hours, and nobody would come.'

It was a close household and an art-loving one. Lauren did a fine art degree and is now an art teacher and printmaker. His mother draws beautifully and paints in oils, and is responsible for all the decorative flourishes around the nursery. And his dad, a retired tiler, is good with his hands. Dean himself did an art foundation course before going to Northumbria University, where he learned skills like lino cutting, book making, silkscreen printing, etching and cyanotypes. 'But it was the relief cuts that I really got into,' he says, with particular inspiration coming from the early twentieth-century woodcuts by German Expressionists and Mexican revolutionary artists.

While in Newcastle, he volunteered at Ouseburn Farm, a city farm focused on therapeutic horticulture, working with a range of people from school kids up to adults, and something clicked. Once he graduated, he went 'WWOOFing' (World Wide Opportunities on Organic Farms) in Poland, and this solidified a growing wish to qualify in horticulture.

'Going forward, I'd like to create a living catalogue, so people can see how the plants will grow in their gardens.'

A tutor on his course saw his artistic sensibilities and recommended reading the books of Christopher Lloyd and Beth Chatto, and for the next four years, as he moved around various jobs, working at Ouseburn Farm, a community garden in Leicester and a social enterprise on Sheffield allotments, he developed an insistent urge to work at their famous gardens.

After eighteen months on the Dixter waiting list, he got his chance with a six-week studentship, and then another at the Beth Chatto Gardens, which he achieved with a canny, here's-what-I-can-do-for-you approach. 'I knew they had a static caravan on site, so I applied as an independent student and told them, "For a small stipend and free accommodation, I'll work my socks off for you." What should have been a three-week placement ended up lasting six months.' They were tough months, though, all through autumn and winter in a caravan with one small radiator. 'It was quite hard, but I loved it. Having the garden to myself after hours was incredible.'

There were other high points he could never have imagined, such as an audience with the queen of horticulture herself, legendary nurserywoman and gardener Beth, who was still alive at the time. 'I started doing lino prints of the garden and I was called in by Beth, as she wanted to see one. It was such an honour to be sat with her – she was like royalty to me. I did prints of the dry garden, her house, the water garden and the woodland garden, and I gave her the first of each edition.'

The amazing experiences didn't end there. A second, supposed three-month stint at Dixter turned into three years working in the garden with another legend, head gardener Fergus Garrett, practising high horticulture and mingling with people from all over the world, from visiting students to the specialist nurseries that came to the garden's famous spring and autumn plant fairs.

And so it might have continued except for the Covid lockdowns, when Dean got furloughed and then called back in to Dixter's nursery to help with the boom in online plant orders. Once things eased, however, he stayed there with nursery lead Michael Morphy, who has run the show for more than twenty years.

Dean learned all the ins and outs of traditional propagation and, due to his previous experience in the garden, was able to work as a sort of middleman between the two, understanding both worlds. 'So when they were, say, lifting plants in the High Garden, I would go up and discuss it, or even put my name down for something ahead of time that we might want to sell. It was a nice symbiotic kind of relationship.'

This behind-the-scenes aspect is a key part of another creative passion: the theatre. He has played baddies and love interests on stage, and worked backstage on various local productions. 'I love knowing how it all works: doing the rigging, the set, the changeovers. This business is seasonal, so "am dram" is good for the wintertime. You need those kinds of activities to stay sane, as it can be a sad time for gardeners. It gives you an uplift.'

Dean has also continued with his black-and-white lino prints wherever he has gone, seeking out print rooms to work at, selling his work online and at fairs, both as personal expression and as an extra income stream. Over time his style has morphed from political statements to pastoral reflections of gardens and landscapes, but always retaining the thread of visually energetic skies – like William Kentridge meets Van Gogh.

His most recent work includes a print of those three beautiful espalier pears and the entrance archway to the nursery, resplendent with its new 'stone' plinth. This is actually a clever 3D-printed polystyrene block designed by Dean – a classy-looking piece to fool passersby until it's possible to afford the real thing. So indecipherable is it as a fake that visiting builders have been known to suck their teeth and declare how it must have cost a pretty penny.

The plinth demonstrates how Dean has to achieve his dream on a shoestring – and all the more impressive for it. But underneath the artistry and effort lies an uncomfortable, niggling question: can a specialist plant nursery work in a town like Rotherham, without the salubrious, garden-mad clientele of more southern counties?

Dean, who hasn't taken a day off or holiday since signing the lease, admits he's put everything into the venture. 'All my savings went into this. We're not rich; we're a working-class

FACING The renovated glasshouse is the engine of the nursery, where Dean propagates all the plants for the business.

N. F. COOPER LTD (FRAMPTON)
no admittance

family taking a huge risk. There are no investors, and the team is just me and Dad, with some volunteers. But I think of it like the film *Field of Dreams* – "If you build it, they will come."'

He hopes to appeal to the holy trinity of nursery customers: the plant geeks who want unusual, rare gems with unpronounceable Latin names, the stable population of gardeners who want good 'doers', and the instant gratification, once-a-year buyers who are drawn to anything in flower. 'It is a huge mix of people,' he admits, 'and that's why I've put common names as well as Latin names on the labels.'

There's not enough money to survive by selling plants alone, he explains, especially when you're up against the budget supermarkets. To make it work, you have to be pragmatic, practical and local. Dean reuses literally everything. He's determined to renovate all the old sheds, despite his father's protestations about the pointlessness of this (after which Glenn happily fixes them up with pride). The huge walnut tree that fell by the old water tank? Leave it exactly as it is – almost an art installation. Those lovely big chunks of stone uncovered last winter? Now an enviable set of steps.

The old greenhouses, too, mostly devoid of glass, are ripe for renewal, starting with the lean-to model that runs along the wall by the entryway. They took it back down to the brickwork and reconstructed it as almost their first job. 'That's the engine room of the nursery; we needed to get that done so propagation could begin, as our main priority. Luckily, my cousins are joiners, roofers and plasterers, and my dad can do anything. Family comes in handy. Mum comes and does some potting on, and Lauren is my business manager. I'm so lucky to have them.'

FACING TOP The infrastructure of old glasshouses was a blessing for Dean and his dad, but they require a lot of repair to get back to full working order. **FACING BOTTOM** Dean's 'skip' walls, carefully compiled from old stone, brick, bottles, logs and anything else he has recovered from the site. **TOP LEFT** The old fallen walnut tree has been left in place and is quite the conversation starter. **TOP RIGHT** The emblem of Hooton's Walled Nursery on the potting shed door.

CASH
WELCOME
CARDS ACCEPTED

Dean collected special plants for years from the Dixter plant fairs and luminaries such as Elizabeth Strangman, and these treasures form the basis of the nursery's stock. All the plants are propagated and grown on site, with no chemicals and with an eye to what's best for biodiversity. Dean knows that provenance is becoming as important for savvy gardeners as for foodies.

When it comes to propagation, there's nothing written down – it's all in his head – but he has his system down to a tee, including making his own peat-free potting compost. 'That's the most important thing for a nursery – getting your mix right. I have never used peat, so I don't know any different, to be honest.' He sells mostly hardy 'garden-worthy' perennials, though Glenn loves succulents, agaves and tropical-looking plants like bananas, and Dean is happy to indulge him.

The site is large, with much ground within the walls still to tame, but Dean is bursting with plans. 'Going forward, I'd like to create a living catalogue, so people can see how the plants will grow in their gardens.' The ideas come flooding out in an intoxicating, giddy mix: an amphitheatre for summer concerts and plays, a tea shed with an honesty box where people can make their own brew, pick-your-own-cut-flowers events, and folksy happenings such as May Day celebrations and January wassailing with Morris dancers.

He wants to make this place a destination, community hub and inspirational space: in an echo of his days in therapeutic horticulture, somewhere that people come back to again and again, feel part of and belong to. It's only the beginning of the story for Hooton's, but you can tell that with the warmth, dedication and passion of Dean and his family, it can't but succeed.

PREVIOUS Dean under the entrance arch of the nursery, which is topped with his new 'stone' plinth. **ABOVE LEFT** Trays of plant pots are laid out with labels that have both common and Latin names on them. **ABOVE RIGHT** The working areas of the nursery are closed to visitors but exceptions can be made. **FACING** The ancient espalier pear trees were one of the special finds that drew Dean to the old nursery.

ERROL REUBEN FERNANDES

AT THE HORNIMAN Museum & Gardens in south London, head of horticulture Errol Reuben Fernandes and his team are busy moving enormous tree ferns into the sheltered courtyard by the entrance. The relocation of the Prehistoric Garden is the latest in a series of big moves Errol has made at the 6.7 hectare (16.5 acre) garden since he started in 2021. The site is visited by almost a million people a year, and both the gardens and the museum's collections of natural history and anthropology are free for all to enjoy.

Errol's role combines many facets, from creating beautiful planting schemes to community building, and is a culmination of everything he has done in his wide-ranging career. He always wanted to work in the creative arts and studied fine art, specializing in painting, at university. Then a week's work experience on style and culture magazines *The Face* and *Dazed & Confused* led to him becoming an assistant fashion stylist and working for *Dazed* co-founder, the lauded photographer Rankin, as a photography assistant.

It was exciting work and came with a party lifestyle. 'Every day there was another famous person strutting around the office, and models everywhere.' But he got tired of reframing other people's ideas. 'I wanted to be an innovator, a creator; to dream up my own stuff.'

While working at *Dazed*, Errol continued to paint, eventually finding rare success, gaining commissions and obtaining gallery representation. His art – multidisciplinary and impressionistic – includes colourful dreamscape paintings and, more recently, sculpture using unearthed broken porcelain.

Errol also led collaborative art outreach projects with galleries and museums, such as the Tate and the V&A, and organizations such as the Metropolitan Police, working with schools, young offenders and teachers on access and inclusion initiatives. Witnessing the transformative effect of making art steered him towards doing a masters degree in art psychotherapy and becoming a therapist for at-risk youth.

He liked to get outside and do garden therapy with his charges, as opposed to sitting in the closed environment of a therapy room. Soon, his practice spread to beyond the garden, to walking along the canals or underpasses where there was graffiti – 'places on the fringes, because a preened garden is probably not where these young people would feel a sense of connection'.

It brought back memories of a brownfield site he used to play in as a child. He remembers the thrill of cycling about with his best friend and discovering the abandoned Victorian dump full of brambles, broken crockery and burnt-out cars. 'My brother suffered with childhood depression, and it wasn't always easy to be at home. This wasteland was a true escape, a wonderland. There was a slight sense of danger and sleaze about the place, which only added to the intrigue.'

It was a place that could contain his anger at the situation he faced at home, but also offer a sense of wonder, through the diversity of exotic plants. 'I remember a datura flower, the cup and saucer vine, and the sickly sweet scent of Himalayan balsam mingling with the fetid smell of stagnant ponds. If I ever get that waft in the air now, it takes me back to that place.

'We'd go there and spend a whole day digging or climbing trees, swimming in the quarry and making dens and fires. We felt like we owned the place. I still have a very powerful connection with it. It's rare that you get to feel that free in a landscape, and it has stayed with me ever since. It's one of the reasons I'm a horticulturist.'

As a therapist, spending time on walks and in the garden also made him realize how much he still loved plants. His mother was a florist, and Errol and his family had gardened together and visited gardens regularly when he was young.

'But it felt like gardening wasn't a career option. It felt stuffy and old-fashioned, and it just was not an aspiration for a young guy, or certainly not this one. There were signals coming from society that this isn't for you. It felt like there was no way in. It's amazing today, with such a diverse, cool cross-section of people in the industry, and I can see there is a space for me; but back then, I couldn't.'

With Errol's interest in plants reignited, he embarked on a part-time horticulture course, where he found a sense of belonging. 'I discovered my people at horticultural college. I was as excited about the craft of gardening as everyone else in the class.'

And then, everything changed for Errol. His brother Terry, who often struggled with his mental health, died. 'When I lost Terry, there was a shift, a sense of urgency for my own future. It became clear that I no longer wanted or needed to be a therapist anymore.' He pivoted to a career in gardening, applying for traineeships and jobs, but the opportunities always seemed to go to someone else. 'I was at the top of my class, had aced all the courses, but I wasn't getting anywhere.' He wondered whether employers were struggling to perceive someone who looked like him in the roles he was applying for. 'Perhaps I wasn't white enough, not posh enough. It was such a frustrating time, but I was encouraged to persevere. I owe so much to my tutor David Francis and to the guidance of some wonderful industry professionals.'

Ultimately, Errol did get a trainee position at the Chelsea Physic Garden in London, but progressing in his horticultural career continued to be a challenge. 'I tried to tell myself that it's the competitive nature of the industry, but I knew it wasn't just that.'

ABOVE Errol editing the Grassland Garden in the autumn to extend the seasonal display. **FACING** The Xerophytic Garden at the front of the museum grows in recycled substrate, featuring a range of arid-loving plants from Mediterranean climate zones.

He worked as a maintenance gardener for a garden designer for a year before getting a job as senior gardener at Kenwood House, an English Heritage property in north London. 'But making the transition to a head gardener role seemed impossibly difficult. It's not about my skill, knowledge, experience, talent, ability or passion. There's still more that needs to change for people like me to feel accepted in those spaces.'

This is part of the reason he said yes to presenting the Channel 4 TV programme *The Great Garden Revolution*, for which he came in for some stick from friends and colleagues. 'There are a lot of people who wondered why I was doing a garden makeover show. I feel like we can all sit on the fringes and say there's not enough diversity in the industry, or we can actually get actively involved and start to inspire people, and be the difference.'

There was a real shift for him in being offered the top role at the Horniman. 'I can think quite dynamically with this organization to make changes, and we can do projects that reflect the diversity of the community in the surrounding areas.'

One of his first new projects in the garden was the microforest, a super dense planting of young trees on a strip of land alongside the busy road that edges the garden. Inspired by a Japanese ecologist called Akira Miyawaki, who pioneered this system to quickly create small resilient woodlands in urban areas, Errol planted nine hundred trees, just 40 centimetres (16 inches) apart, in only 400 square metres (4,300 square feet).

From tiny pencil-thick saplings, in just a few years the young trees have already grown taller than him. Although Miyawaki's method usually uses local and native trees, Errol has mixed it up with thirty-five different species, including oak, ash and silver birch but also spindle, dogwoods, wild service trees and pines. 'We've selected for bud break, blossom, foraging, for animals and people as well as autumn colour, so there's a lot of successional interest throughout the entire year.'

It's a system that is directly inspired by the way that natural forests develop, encouraging competitive growth and,

PREVIOUS The Sunken Garden contains diverse, multi-seasonal, layered planting with trees, shrubs and perennials such as *Sorbus vilmorinii*, *Rosa glauca*, *Symphyotrichum* and *Solidago rugosa*. **FACING** An exciting range of edible plants under a row of old olive trees, including Mediterranean herbs, cavolo nero, *Amaranthus* 'Fat Spike', tomatillo and scrambling squash. **ABOVE** Rows of Grade II listed terracing provide a wonderful vantage point to enjoy the Sunken Garden.

'I feel like we can all sit on the fringes and say there's not enough diversity in the industry, or we can actually get actively involved and start to inspire people.'

eventually an interconnected community of trees that, through crossing and self-seeding, will develop resilience.

Another area Errol has developed is at the front of the sandstone museum building, under the lofty clocktower, with beds of drought-tolerant, xerophytic planting. South-facing and sun-baked, it was the perfect spot to grow plants from all over the planet, in line with founder Sir Frederick Horniman's wish to bring the world to Forest Hill.

The idea was sparked by 25 tonnes of hardcore, rubble, gravel and concrete left over from a major pathway project on site. Rather than send it to landfill, Errol banked it up to use as a free-draining substrate. The plants, including silver-leaved stalwarts such as euphorbias and sea kale, have low water needs and are more likely to manage high summer temperatures. It now has a Mediterranean feel and helps to underline the effects of climate change.

It was a different proposition when it came to bringing the Arts and Crafts style Sunken Garden, designed in the 1930s, into the modern era. Terraces of benches look down into the space, which has a rectangular pond at its centre and previously featured gaudy bedding displays. These tender plants are usually grown en masse in heated greenhouses, often with chemicals, and put on a show for just a short window of time, which didn't sit right with Errol or the museum's remit of sustainability.

'No one can deny the visual spectacle bedding has,' says Errol. 'But you have to understand what's below the surface of that colourful display, what it's taken to achieve in carbon, water, time and money.' He wanted to create an immersive feeling without the waste, and make sure the space was boosting biodiversity. So the team made the pond deeper, and switched to, first, more easy-going annuals such as cosmos for long-lasting, pollinator-friendly displays, and they are now transitioning the space over to perennial plants.

Other areas in the garden include a grassland prairie, designed in collaboration with Professor James Hitchmough before Errol came on board, with North American and South African plants known to have been used by indigenous peoples. But even here Errol has made his mark, cutting the lignified stems of the flowers and grasses in late winter to make artful 'bug snugs', with bunches tied to chestnut stakes to provide cover and food for invertebrates.

Much of the lawned area in the wider garden, formerly mowed short, has now been developed into a wildflower meadow, and in the parkland the grass is left to grow long in summer. Errol has expanded his group of garden volunteers to forty, and even introduced an annual plant fair, to much excitement from city-bound gardeners.

Previously the museum's gardens were developed in the same way that a curator might shape an internal display or temporary exhibition, but Errol has taken a different approach, making sure he is informed by the mission and collections of the Horniman, but pushing for wider-reaching, more permanent developments and initiatives.

'My team and I are able to develop new ideas and work to take the garden forward. There's so much creative expression within the garden, with structure, form, colour and movement – it's almost like a moving painting.' But unlike a painting, he says, this garden doesn't stand still, and it is open all the time, for everyone, not just hanging on the wall of the one person wealthy enough to own it.

Errol may have swapped paint for plants, but he still identifies first and foremost as an artist, using the garden to demonstrate and communicate important concepts and ideas. He baulks at using words like 'vocation' or 'calling', but it's clear this is more than a job to him.

'It feels like I need to be doing this. The garden is like a long-term giant art installation, and creatively very fulfilling. As an artist, I didn't just paint for myself. I painted for criticism, for the pleasure of others, to evoke a response. Creating a garden in the public realm is no different. I want to produce work that challenges people and provides moments of beauty. If we can inspire people to love nature, then maybe they'll look after it.'

FACING Errol takes an artistic and collaborative approach to the garden, encouraging creative expression and innovation amongst his team and volunteers, and a playful connection with their visitors.

CHARLOTTE MOLESWORTH

'YOU CAN NEVER have enough topiary,' says Charlotte Molesworth. Looking out across her garden, where bobble-headed box shapes vie for attention with peacock-topped yew dumplings and spiralled cones of bay, it's clear this is a credo she lives by.

The artist-gardener and her husband, Donald, have been crafting the pastoral paradise at Balmoral Cottage in Benenden for more than forty years – a life's work. 'We love the garden. We didn't have children, so this has really become sort of like our child, because we developed it from embryonic stages with cuttings from my mother's garden, and my aunt's and friends'.'

Charlotte is an original, just like her garden. A farmer's daughter, she was encouraged to draw by her mother, who loved to paint and garden, and went to art school in Canterbury before getting a job in London at Foyle's Bookshop, despite not being very bookish. 'My boss took pity on me because I was a fish out of water. Her husband was a tailor at the Royal Opera House, and they helped me find a place in the dye department.'

Everything at the theatre was eye-openingly different and exciting. Part of her role was to watch all the productions, and she spent three years working on costumes and props for performers including ballet dancer Rudolf Nureyev. She went on to train as a teacher and taught art at Benenden School, a private boarding school for girls, for many years, meeting Donald in a local pub along the way.

'We met through mutual friends – an art school friend of mine and a farming college friend of his. We sat rather apart on this table, and then Donald moved next to me and said, "I'd love to see you again." We hadn't known each other very long when he asked if I would marry him. I was delighted, but he sort of surprised me, so I said, "Crumbs, I'd better take some box cuttings." Because I knew that wherever we ended up, we'd make a garden.' So focused were they on the dream of their future garden, they even asked friends and family for box cuttings and self-sown yew seedlings for wedding presents.

Donald had shifted from farming to gardening, taking a job restoring the grounds of The Grange, the Victorian house and garden previously owned by the famous Collingwood 'Cherry' Ingram. An expert in Japanese ornamental cherries, Ingram was responsible for reintroducing the lost great white cherry, *Prunus* 'Tai-haku', back to Japan. He had died a couple of years prior in 1981 at the ripe age of 101, and his estate had become neglected in places, including the old kitchen garden with its gardener's bothy and pigsty.

'It was a sleeping beauty,' says Charlotte, 'the most romantic, unimaginably beautiful overgrown jungle with cabbages and leeks flowering everywhere.' There were gnarly old apple trees and some fine pines Ingram had planted as a shelter belt, but it was essentially a blank canvas with beautifully cultivated soil – what more could you ask for when starting a garden?

Balmoral Cottage, on the other hand, was small and almost derelict, with a leaking roof, wonky foundations, bad wiring, one meagre lightbulb and just a Rayburn stove for warmth, but the couple were so enchanted that they approached Donald's employers, the Millers, to ask if they could buy it.

Donald had inherited some money following his father's death, but it still wasn't enough and the building society was not inclined to help – 'They went, "Ha, ha, ha, we're not giving you a mortgage on that wreck."' So the Millers kindly offered to lend them the rest, meaning that for years Donald's wages

looped straight back to them, and the couple lived solely on Charlotte's part-time teaching salary.

The newlyweds moved in on Christmas Eve 1983, with just a bed, a table and two chairs, plus their dogs, cats, chickens and a donkey called Mrs Watson. Charlotte set about planting out her box and yew babies in rows to grow on, like a mini nursery, and over time she clipped these bushes and hedges into a wonderment of bewilderingly brilliant shapes.

There are waves and swags, poodle-form lollipops and abstract multi-tiered stacks, as well as birds, dogs and foxes. She has previously made a lion and a bear as well a porcupine – most challenging due to the direction of the spikes. 'You have to get to know your specimen – your victim,' she says, detailing how she shapes each topiary. 'This one' – she points to a tall chess piece by the terrace – 'was always right from the very beginning, with the most marvellous straight central trunk. A beautiful little plant and all the branches came off it laterally. Whereas the birds have to have a much more shrubby sort of bushy character to begin with.'

She is even now much in demand to clip forms at other gardens and teach people how to do what she does. 'They don't see what's inside a shrub when it's just a blob. Most people are completely clueless about that stuff.' You're the shrub whisperer, I tell her, able to see the shape it can become. She sketches out a form on paper, indicating with big sweeps of her marker how a bush could be approached, cut back and moulded, and it does all seem so simple, until, with shears in hand, you stand before a real-life shrub looking to make those cuts. 'You have to be bold and cut out some quite serious bits of wood.' And don't worry about messing up, she advises. 'It's so forgiving – it grows back.'

Box may have fallen out of favour with most gardeners now thanks to pests and diseases, but though Charlotte is concerned, she is not swayed in her devotion to it. For the sake of resilience, there are several different *Buxus* species and cultivars growing

PREVIOUS Balmoral Cottage garden is known for the variety of topiary on show, from peacocks to chess pieces. **ABOVE** Charlotte reuses everything from second-hand bricks for paths to pig-swill buckets as planters. **FACING** A lilac bush blooms between the cottage and the old potting shed.

'Friends are key to our time here on this Earth. I often think of what we give back and what we take out and how we use our time.'

FACING TOP LEFT A characterful water pump and basin. **FACING TOP RIGHT** Characterful trees including medlars and willows including *Salix hookeriana* and 'Nancy Saunders' edge the pond. **FACING BOTTOM** Charlotte has mowed a labyrinth of concentric circles in her meadowy lawn, inspired by one made by local landscape designer Marian Boswall. **ABOVE** The silver-variegated leaves of a crown-raised *Cornus alternifolia* 'Argentea' adding bright notes throughout the dark evergreen yew forms.

in the garden, and she continues to take cuttings of interesting forms and varieties where she finds them. Some of the plants at Balmoral do get rust, because of lack of airflow on the flat site and the density of growth due to regular clipping, but so far there has not been a plague of box blight or caterpillars, as she sprays three times a year with a biological control.

Their main issue these days is simply the size of the clipped forms and Charlotte and Donald's advancing age. 'Topiary is useful because you have to do very little to it, but it does grow bigger – one of its main drawbacks. It starts off manageable and then forty years on they become rather out of reach. But we've got good ladders and I do get help now – we always need strong young men in this place,' she says. 'When we made the garden, I never thought of putting in a reverse gear. I got so keen on making more and more topiary, and we got more and more plants. Because we're both hoarders, we're always finding rescues who needed a home.'

She has several hair-raising tales to this effect, including the time she shoved an enormous box tree she found abandoned on the roadside into her Mini and drove it home to Donald with her head poking out the window. But it is not just plants that get a second life at Balmoral, as this is a garden created over time, with patience and ingenuity, on a shoestring. Much of Charlotte's true creative flair can be found in how she recycles things most people would put in a skip.

'This is an age of such shocking waste,' she says. 'Donald and I never had a huge amount of money to chuck about – just enough to get by. You can usually use somebody else's cast-offs, and we love to save things.' Prime examples of her clever repurposing include old animal feeders used as planters, gateposts for table legs, a rubber conveyor belt for pathways and stable blocks for stepping stones.

FACING The white pompon flowers of an unidentified white-flowered viburnum Charlotte inherited when she moved in – an unusual form probably planted by Collingwood Ingram – are a highlight amid the lush layering of planting in this immersive garden. **ABOVE** The meadow to Charlotte's woodland has a path mown through the buttercups and cow parsley.

The bricks in the path that lead from the garden gate to the front door were salvaged from across the garden, and many other elements from gates to seats were found second hand at reclamation sales or donated. They spotted their polytunnel dilapidated on the side of the road when driving past, and bought it for next to nothing. Everything that can be gets composted, even old clothes, and the chickens take care of the rest.

There are also several artful reworkings of structures, such as the summer house converted from a swimming pool changing hut and a greenhouse cobbled together from old windows and doors. The ultimate example is her painting studio, which was formerly a toolshed and piggery and then Mrs Watson the donkey's stable. After the great storm of 1987 took the roof off – 'I slept right through it,' admits Charlotte – and she made some extra money designing garden projects and painting murals, they were able to convert it properly into a workspace for her art.

She mostly uses walnut ink in her work but has recently been experimenting with soil-based stains, making her own pigment from earth gathered under an oak tree to paint studies of that same tree. Each year she holds an open day in the garden and studio to exhibit her work and that of other artists, and lends her brush to various causes such as raising money for the Great Dixter Charitable Trust.

It is possible to lose many hours walking and talking with Charlotte in the garden, feeding the tame sheep, spotting unusual treasures in the borders and strolling round the pond. You know you should be on your way, but stay a bit longer to discuss the provenance of her double-flowered white primulas and admire the grass spiral in her lawn. She and Donald are generous hosts, proffering welcome wine and treats such as fresh cherries and homegrown artichokes to even unexpected visitors with delighted ease.

'Friends are key to our time here on this Earth,' she says. 'I often think of what we give back and what we take out and how we use our time. You've got to look at it quite laterally sometimes, and think, crumbs, we really have to make the most of it.'

ABOVE Inside Charlotte's studio, which looks out over the garden, she often makes her own pigments to paint with. **FACING** She has created and tended the extraordinary topiary yew forms and wavy box hedges from tiny cuttings for decades.

KATY MERRINGTON

FOLLOW KATY MERRINGTON on social media and you're sure to see one of her occasional videos portraying elements of her role as cultural gardener at The Hepworth Wakefield gallery. Whether it's showing off her pimped-up hand pallet truck in the style of *Top Gear* or reading someone's dropped shopping list as a surrealist poem, these humorous nuggets give a small window into her wonderfully whimsical mindset.

Wakefield is an old Victorian mill town in West Yorkshire, famous for being the birthplace of world-renowned twentieth-century sculptor Barbara Hepworth. The gallery, named in her honour, is set beside the windy River Calder, surrounded by an industrial estate and bound at one end by a busy road junction with six lanes of roaring traffic.

It's not a situation you'd typically expect to find a stunning new piece of landscape design – described by its creator, designer Tom Stuart-Smith, as a living composition – but this unlikely site is now home to a free public garden of almost an acre which, radically, is open to all 24/7, 365 days a year.

The garden sits between the gallery designed by starchitect David Chipperfield – a series of offset trapezoidal concrete boxes of different sizes – and the old Rutland Mills building with its traditional red-brick walls and arched windows. Owned by the council, the site had just been laid to a drab rectangle of lawn for the previous ten years, so the gallery team suggested they could do something more interesting that would benefit the wider community.

Tom's studio won the competition to design the space with a planting plan that would offer colour all through the year in several peaks, including tulips and daffodils in spring and prairie perennials in high summer. Asymmetric planting beds of irregular shapes vaguely echo the idea of the blocks of the gallery building, but with more organic, rounded edges, and narrow concrete paths run through, swelling into dwelling spots where they interconnect. Seen from the ceiling-high gallery windows above, it's like a contemporary patchwork quilt.

To minimize the view and noise of the busy road at the far end of the plot, Tom specified a 4.4 metre- (14 foot-) high concrete wall; he may be the only person who could make such an intervention look stylish. This grey slab mimics the gallery walls, bookends the garden, and offers a neutral backdrop to the first of three planting zones: the woodland edge. Shady and mostly green, it features several pin oak trees as well as amelanchier and prunus, which offer blossom in spring and colourful autumn foliage.

Tom always makes sure to include shrubs in his designs, and across the garden there are some of his signature picks, including multi-stemmed *Rhus typhina* and flowering dogwood as well as philadelphus and cotinus.

The middle, open area of the garden is the complex meadow zone, with wilder, dynamic planting of herbaceous perennials and ornamental grasses, including spires of purple loosestrife, pink coneflower, pale blue wands of Russian sage, zingy lime euphorbia, and pennisetum and hakonechloa grasses. There are several *Malus* 'Evereste' trees that give blossom in spring and crab apples in autumn, and three small lawns dotted through as spaces for the eye and visitors to rest.

The third planting zone, nearest to the gallery entrance and surrounding a small plaza for gathering by the summer cafe building, is a mix of the two previous styles. Dotted through the space there are sculptures by Barbara Hepworth, Kim Lim, Halima Cassell and Michael Craig-Martin.

Beds are bordered along some edges with low beech hedges, like cradling arms that protect the plants from the stomped-over corners commonly seen in public parks – indeed, Katy calls these hedges 'steel toecaps' for the beds. They also help to create a sense of discovery on this small flat site, hiding and revealing each area in turn as you walk through.

Katy came on board as the garden was being built, and the planting was completed just as the Covid lockdowns hit. The novel idea of being a gardener of a gallery appealed to her, as a callback to her years studying fine art at university and trying to forge a career afterwards doing 'all sorts of funny, weird things' from freelance film making to architectural lighting.

To make ends meet, Katy also did cleaning – 'we called it "housekeeping" so we could charge more,' she laughs – and sometimes got asked to do a client's garden too. 'Around the same time, I also got an allotment, and that's how it started. Gardening took over for me. I was obsessed.'

A couple she cleaned and cared for in old age, retired professors from Oxford, left her a small lump sum in their will, and because they believed in lifelong learning, she felt she should spend it on a course. 'That was how I realized you could study professional gardening.' She started out with the basics on an evening course, swotting up in her car on her lunch breaks, and did some volunteering before applying for every apprenticeship and scheme she could, and was lucky enough to get a place at the National Trust for Scotland's respected School for Heritage Gardening.

Gardening also gave Katy the opportunity to travel. 'I put all my stuff in storage in my grandmother's loft for about five years, and worked in different gardens, sometimes on scholarships or traineeships, for a year at a time.' Her placements included Tresco Abbey on the Isles of Scilly, Longwood Gardens in America, RHS Harlow Carr in Yorkshire and Logan Botanic Garden in Scotland.

PREVIOUS At the end of the garden, a tall concrete wall blocks the sight and sound of the road, and echoes the gallery building. **FACING TOP LEFT** The garden is a strip of land sandwiched between the gallery and the old Rutland Mills buildings. The prairie planting here includes phlomis and Russian sage. **FACING TOP RIGHT** Beds with blocks of fountain grass and hakonechloa form the outer edge of the garden. **FACING BOTTOM** Pink *Echinacea pallida* and the foliage of amsonia create a swathe that draws the eye to the sculpture *Pitchfork (Yellow)* by Michael Craig-Martin.

She was just trying to figure out her next step when she saw the ad for a cultural gardener at The Hepworth Wakefield. 'I thought it would be fun to be the first gardener of somewhere.' She is the only gardener on staff, and works solo every day, rain and shine, but there are a burgeoning volunteer programme and plans to have a trainee in the future. Tom also comes to visit regularly, and they work in partnership to plan ongoing changes. 'People sometimes wonder if I have a problem with that, but I don't,' she says. 'He's so knowledgeable and I really want to hear what he's got to say. I've never studied garden design, but I think I've learned more than you could on any course by looking after a garden designed by someone who is so good.'

It's commonplace that where a well-known designer has created a space, the credit and glory often reside with them, with less recognition of those who develop and care for the gardens every day. Katy's unusual title of cultural gardener is, perhaps, a way to make people more aware that as well as it being a practical, physical job, there is real artistry and craft to it too.

'Gardening is creative,' she says. 'If you are weeding, for example, you're effectively editing next year's plants, making a series of thoughtful, intelligent decisions. Your brain is having to visualize how big that seedling will be in a year and sometimes that could be 2 metres (7 feet) high, so you're picturing something that doesn't exist yet. You have to be a time-traveller, looking into the future.'

But a garden doesn't have the same insurable, marketable value as a sculpture or painting, meaning you can't sell it for an ever-increasing price, she points out. Maybe that's why gardening isn't held in such high regard as other branches of the arts. 'But it should be, because it's probably harder than any of those other things to do well. Not only have you got a million elements to deal with, but they're alive and changing minute by minute. That's more difficult than carving a sculpture and plonking it in an air-controlled museum.'

Where the garden has the edge over the artwork in the gallery, of course, is how accessible it is not just to visitors but to locals, who can come and enjoy this extraordinary slice of public green space any time they like. It's a different sort of crowd to those Katy experienced when working at open gardens that people pay to enter.

'You're in a conversation with nature, but it's also a constant chase to try to make it how you want it to be, but you can't quite achieve.'

'The garden was built just before the pandemic, and people came here on their daily walks. And we have lots of people who come, particularly older people who might live alone or need exercise, to whom the garden has become very special, so that can be quite moving.'

Katy has run the gamut of social interactions, from men propositioning her to people bringing her choc ices, and has several regulars she sees nearly every day. 'They know th at they can have a chat when they get here, because the garden's small and they look out for me. There are not many places in our society where you can pass the time of day, and these light-touch, loose social connections can entirely transform your sense of well-being – just having someone who knows your name and asks you how you are. You might not speak to anyone else all day, but that would be enough to see you psychologically through. Those chats are very important to people, and it brings the garden to life having a person in it that you can go and see. It makes people feel like there's a community.'

Being open to all at all times does have some drawbacks. Because it has no fences and is not locked, anyone is able to wander in and do whatever they like, from giving unsanctioned garden tours to using it as a free wedding venue – and any of the other less wholesome things you can imagine parks are used for at night.

'But it helps protect the garden that people can see there is someone here every day, making it. It's different causing a mess in the place of someone you know than in a faceless park. It also visually demonstrates the gallery's organizational care; a lot of love goes into an art collection, but it all happens behind closed doors in climate-controlled rooms. Here in the garden, that care and love is visible day in, day out, and that's the power of it.'

Talking with Katy and seeing her dedication to this style of public gardening, it's no surprise to discover that she has received the honour of a British Empire Medal for services to the local community. What other role could be said to combine science, art, culture, ecology and social work in one? And it's obvious that she truly enjoys this part of her job too.

'In my art, I was always into suspension of disbelief, and I realize I'm still interested in this, because that is what gardens do. They say, "Come into this little paradise – it's better here." How they do that, and how much it takes to do that, are questions that interest me. There are no walls or fences to this garden, and it's straight off the road. So how do you set it apart from the world? It's why I feel we have to keep it clean, with no litter, so you feel like you're entering some other oasis.'

The challenges of making this, or any, garden a separate, special place, of course, are all those things that are out of your control. 'You're always on the cusp of thinking this year could be the best it's ever been; and then it falls away from you,' Katy explains. 'You're in a conversation with nature, but it's also a constant chase to try to make it how you want it to be, but you can't quite achieve. So you love it, and you hate it, because you can never get there.' She smiles, happy enough to be foiled by the cycle of the seasons. 'But that's why gardening is addictive – because you're always striving.'

PREVIOUS The red woolly fruits of a multi-stem *Rhus typhina* tree create the backdrop for the bronze sculpture *Ascending Form (Gloria)* by Barbara Hepworth. **FACING** Katy is a constant presence in the garden, talking to new and regular local visitors, creating a sense of community as well as looking after the aesthetic aims of the space.

SING

MATTHEW RICE

MATTHEW RICE, the watercolour artist and illustrator, is best known for the cheerful designs of the British pottery brand founded by him and his ex-wife, Emma Bridgewater. His interests extend to architecture (about which he has published several books), but his heart truly lies in the garden – specifically the garden of his home, Ham Court, which he has created from scratch over the past decade or so.

The house, on the edge of the village of Bampton, was once a castle, started around 1320 but never finished. It was pillaged for stone, reworked and added on to several times over the centuries. 'It's really interesting and odd, but it's no Georgian rectory,' says Matthew.

When they bought the property in 2011, it was a working beef and arable farm with the yard all laid to concrete, full of rubbish and old tyres. It had no garden, and the historic front of the house was blocked by large modern barns. Over time, they dismantled the huge barns one by one and lifted the concrete. Matthew's then brother-in-law ('a sort of earth-moving genius') used a digger to clear the ground and fill in some unfortunate slurry lagoons they found, as well as to carve out an actual moat around the house, as befits a medieval castle.

This single, incredibly bold move defined the new garden by placing a square frame around the inner 1.6 hectares (4 acres). But as well as definition, the water also brought life: families of geese and ducks as well as dragonflies and kingfishers.

The other significant thing Matthew did in those early years was to create the wider landscape, planting shelter belts of trees all the way around the 12 hectare (30 acre) property, to create his dream of a home that was like an island in a wood. The 12,000 trees blocked the sight and sound of the nearby road and drew in birds, butterflies, deer, badgers and foxes, giving him 'a broad, deep backcloth of nature' to build upon.

And build he did. The old farmyard is now a grand entrance courtyard offering a fittingly awe-inspiring approach, showing off the house's striking Cotswold-stone facade, smothered in roses and wisteria, at its best. In front of the house, on the advice of garden designers Isabel and Julian Bannerman, Matthew has created a light, bright gravel garden, which features a smattering of drought-tolerant perennials such as irises as well as planted containers and four sculpted yews. 'It's nice to have somewhere to paddle around immediately outside your house.' In the corner, a large wooden table with mismatched chairs forms the main entertaining space for morning coffee and evening aperitifs.

Through a wooden gate is the walled kitchen garden, the first major area Matthew created, putting it back exactly where it had been on a map from 1790. 'This is first and foremost a productive garden – my thing is growing vegetables and cut flowers. When I go around someone else's garden, I'm always longing to get to the radishes. That's where, for me, the business end of it is.'

He was inspired by the Potager du Roi at Versailles, a baroque kitchen garden created in the seventeenth century and renowned for its beauty as well as its bounty. It is this combination of form and function that drives Matthew in his own plot. 'It's not an allotment, a farm or a market garden. I care what everything looks like,' he admits.

Inside these walls – built bit by bit over many years as and when his finances allowed – vegetables and fruit grow in serried rows, and beds of flowers for cutting bring heady

pops of colour. The big surprises are the perfectly proportioned croquet lawn and a Douglas fir tower in the corner, designed by Matthew to offer a vantage point over the garden, and built by artist-carpenter Gabriel Langlands and Matthew's son Michael.

A long low greenhouse runs along one side, its interior strong with the scent of lilies and sweet peas – a 'noisy symphony of smells'. Even the working areas here have a certain panache; in the dark potting shed along the way, a blackboard features an ordered list of jobs to do, and tools hang neatly on the wall. Matthew might also have the prettiest compost area ever seen, which is looked after mostly by his one full-time gardener, who lives on-site.

Just outside the kitchen garden, a polytunnel brims with more edible beauties – giant cabbages and tomato plants dripping with fruit. 'Even though a polytunnel is not a thing of beauty, this is the bit that does it for me,' he says. 'I know no nicer place.'

On the opposite side of the house, the Victorian wing, is one of Matthew's only flower borders, with an all-pink colour scheme and a huge weeping willow at one end. The south-facing area beside it was previously very bumpy croquet lawn, but recently a large area has been allowed to grow out into a meadow, with 'Mutabilis' roses scattered through. Within a few years, they will create beautiful mounds of shifting colour among the long grass in summer, as the butterfly-like petals age from honeyed gold to a rich reddy-pink.

This 'wild and woolly' area is contained with a boundary of rusty-hued estate fencing. 'It stitches up the edges of things, like hemming a quilt.' More roses clamber up the railings – in time they will lend a sense of lost romance to the scene, perfectly in keeping with the 'informal country' style Matthew is aiming for.

In the broader landscape in and around the moat, there are green allées of hornbeam, rows of pollarded willows, orchards of old varieties of apple trees and a second kitchen garden, where sunflowers grow between the feathery fronds of asparagus – an idea, he admits, ripped straight from the kitchen garden at Petworth House in Sussex. 'I'm always seeing things and thinking, oh, I'll put that into the compost heap that is my mind, and hope that it will turn up at some point and be a useful thing to add in.'

PREVIOUS The walled kitchen garden of Ham Court is the productive heart of the whole garden and Matthew's passion. **FACING TOP** Rows of salad, squash, potatoes, and beans fill the immaculately tended beds. **FACING BOTTOM** In the greenhouse Matthew grows bright pelargoniums, sweet peas and exquisitely scented lilies. **ABOVE** The artist has trained plants such as figs on the walls of the outbuildings.

'I always draw from real life, not photographs. I want to capture the feeling of the plant, the spirit of it. Flowers are joyous, alive things.'

FACING The table in the front gravel garden is laid for tea with Emma Bridgewater pottery and a saucepan and urn overflowing with cut flowers. Beyond, the woooden pavilion gives a second level view over the garden. **ABOVE AND LEFT** The long grass meadow has been planted with several 'Mutabilis' roses, which Matthew hopes will start to spread and sprawl throughout in a romantic fashion.

Like most gardeners, Matthew has begged, borrowed and stolen ideas over the years, but his key garden aspirations have been the same since he was young and would do drawings of the house he wanted to live in, with a garden and fields and barns and animals. 'This garden is a response to an idea I developed in my teenage years of how I might live, when I ought to have been doing proper teenage activities. I was endlessly growing better broad beans and things like that. I've always been a gardener. I had a tiny garden when I was a child full of little ponds and rocks.'

He grew up in a house where everybody drew all day. His father, Peter Rice, created sets for operas, ballets and plays, and his mother, Pat Albeck, designed textiles. 'There was no sitting room – there were two studios,' he explains. He went to art school to do theatre design, following his father, but didn't design for the stage 'for more than about ten seconds'.

This training has, however, had a big influence on his approach to garden design. 'It's not theatrical in terms of making great bold wild statements, but I definitely make a series of sets. I am all the time trying to make places that have interesting views through from one place to another. I think about how one bit relates to the other, and having an interesting progression as you walk around, because that's how you experience gardens.'

On any tour of the garden, Matthew's two black Labradors are always by his side. Sheep and goats graze in the surrounding fields, and chickens cluck about here and there. 'In making the set, they're my actors.'

It may be his living stage, but most importantly, the garden is a direct tool and feed for his work, as a source of subjects to paint and as the setting for his botanical painting courses. In the light, high-ceilinged studio – a converted old stone barn just across from the house – dressers are stacked with his archive of

FACING Climbing roses clamber around the windows of the house, which features sections from different eras. **ABOVE** The moat runs around the property, enclosing three sides of the house. The wider estate includes woodland and meadows.

Bridgewater mugs, teapots, jugs and plates, featuring designs drawn directly from the garden. There are pots of paint, brushes and stacks of paper, vases stuffed with posies and piles of books. Framed tea towels designed by his mother line the walls, and paper birds in various states of flight dangle and twirl above.

Matthew digs out a painting of some poppies he has been trying to capture, and speaks of waiting weeks to paint unfurling irises, only to be too busy to do them when they finally appeared. 'I always draw from real life, not photographs. I want to capture the feeling of the plant, the spirit of it. Flowers are joyous, alive things.'

Matthew encourages his students to follow his lead and observe their subjects in person. 'Designers, particularly at the moment, spend their lives looking at a screen, and it's easy not to be open to other influences. You have to get up from your desk and go and see the thing in three dimensions, and see how deep it is and all around it. When you're looking in books or on your phone as a reference, it's not good enough.'

As well as being his muse and workshop, the garden also functions as a venue for the circus Fool's Delight, run by his daughter, with the Big Top up and an influx of performers practising their moves among the lettuces and dahlias. In fact, he seems to delight in finding every way to fill the garden with as many people as possible. 'It comes to life for me when it's full of people. I walk around and there are people sitting on all the benches and lurking around corners and chatting and looking at things, and I think, yes . . . it's being used.'

As fun as it all sounds, and as much as he plays the *bon vivant*, Matthew grows serious when it comes to the garden. He speaks of getting up at 5 a.m. to garden for three hours before anyone else rises, and it's clear he works extremely hard to make the garden a place of ease and, as he says only half-jokingly, 'idle leisure' for those who visit.

'It's the third garden I've made, and it might be the last – who knows? Each time you get a bit nearer to what you want. It's been a continuous process, and I quite like change,' he says. 'I think it's fun to keep on doing stuff.'

ABOVE Matthew's designs displayed on a dresser in his studio.
FACING Matthew is in the garden every minute he can, often rising early to work in the kitchen garden.

BEX PARTRIDGE

PEOPLE HAVE CALLED Bex Partridge's extraordinary floral creations magical, ethereal, organic and intriguing. The dried flower artist chooses the word 'contemporary': 'I try very hard to stay away from the traditional, because I want to change people's perception of dried flowers as dusty old things your granny had in her house.'

Her style is sculptural, with natural architecture from branches and texture from seed heads. 'It's all been self-taught. A lot of it comes down to play and experimentation,' she says. 'Often it's inspired by a particular material that I want to work with, such as dried bamboo, and then that will inform me making something. But it's always about bringing the outside in.'

Plants have been a constant in her life – she used to spend her pocket money buying plants for her mother's garden. 'And when my friends were all clubbing in London, I wanted to come home and tend my sweet peas.' And yet, she took a long and roundabout route to working with her passion.

Bex left school at sixteen and trained to be a chef, working with a catering company doing weddings and dinner parties for several years. After a stint travelling, she studied for a degree at night and managed to land a marketing role at the multinational Unilever in Leatherhead, Surrey. She ended up moving to Amsterdam with her husband, Ed, for two years, where she was inspired by the wild-style floral displays people created for their front windows. 'It definitely sparked what I'm doing now.'

On returning to the UK, with her first son still a baby, Bex tried to reduce her working hours. 'The job was never right for me, and looking back now, I can see how deeply unhappy I was most of the time. Then I had a really awful miscarriage, and immediately fell pregnant again, which meant I was pregnant for almost fourteen months. I was never diagnosed but I think that, afterwards, I had postnatal depression.'

They had just moved to a property built on the grounds of an old manor house. In spring, while she was on maternity leave with her second son and struggling with her mental health, the old garden came to life. 'There were so many amazing flowers coming up, and I needed something good to focus on, so I focused on the flowers. I set up an Instagram account, my idea being that I just wanted to share what I was witnessing and experiencing.'

She saw flowers grown for drying on an allotment one day, wondered if she could grow them too and what she could do with them, and Botanical Tales was born. 'The thing that started the business was wreaths,' she says. 'Everyone loves a wreath. And the great thing about dried flowers is that you can send them anywhere – they travel well, so my audience is pretty wide.'

She also makes flower garlands and bouquets, larger pieces like flower 'clouds', and custom installations for private homes, restaurants and stores, as well as running online and in-person workshops. It's mostly seasonal, so Bex opens her online shop for orders in autumn and works tirelessly through winter and into spring. 'Summer is a quiet time for my business, when I gather inspiration.'

At the start, Bex was still working in her corporate job, but this became untenable. 'Everyone was telling me that I was a huge success, but I was not feeling it. It got to the point where working full-time and doing this thing on the side, plus having two young children, was not great for the family or me. I wanted to be more present for my kids and to do what I love. When

'The beauty of growing flowers to dry is how many butterflies there are, because I'm not cutting the blooms when they're in bud, but after they have opened.'

ABOVE Bex let the grass grow long and cut a path through it to her studio. To one side is one of her greenhouses and on the other is a treehouse for her sons. **FACING** The cutting garden in summer with red poppies, white bladder campion and rustic wigwams covered in sweet peas.

I finally quit, I felt very free. It was like I'd been living someone else's life.'

She had saved enough to live on for a while, so was able to nurture the fledgling business and experiment. Then the Covid lockdown happened, and her first book, *Everlastings*, was published. People stuck at home with time on their hands and a creative itch seized upon her advice and the idea of dried flowers, and things really started to take off. Soon after, the family moved from suburban Surrey to coastal Lyme Regis in an effort to simplify their lives, to an eco-house surrounded by nature, close to the woods and the sea.

Bex now works in a new studio in her garden that she crowdfunded and her husband built. It is light and airy – just right for drying flowers – with a long horizontal window across the back wall that overlooks the neighbouring wildflower meadow. To one side of the studio are her boys' treehouse and a strip of lawn where they play football. Bex has left much of the rest of the grass to grow long.

Her growing plot beyond is framed with charmingly rustic homemade fencing to keep out the deer, rabbits and her cluck-happy chickens. Colourful strawflowers, lacy *Ammi majus*, spires of larkspur and fluffy grasses mingle with stands of sweet peas, marjoram and dahlias, as well as nigella, mallow and poppies grown for their seed heads.

The flowers rub shoulders with peas and cucumbers, raspberries, blackcurrants and gooseberries; by the greenhouse there are mini ponds that have attracted baby newts and dragonflies. 'It brings me so much joy to stand in this space. I don't grow in straight lines. I shove it all in and invariably it ends up looking beautiful. There's no space left and no cohesive look, but somehow it sort of works.'

On sunny days, the beds come alive with pollinators. 'The beauty of growing flowers to dry is how many butterflies there are, because I'm not cutting the blooms when they're in bud, but after they have opened,' Bex explains.

As well as her garden, she has two allotments nearby, but she still can't grow everything she needs, so she leans on a network of local flower farmers to supplement what she produces.

There's a second greenhouse by her studio for sowing seeds and a charming shingle shack further along, as well as a black-clad annexe with its own deck – built around two existing fruit trees in another light-touch intervention.

Bex grows most of her perennials in curving flower borders by the house, including scabious, achillea and her absolute favourite, the plume poppy (*Macleaya cordata*). Around the back is an outdoor dining area overhung with a beautiful ginkgo tree and surrounded by mature sheltering shrubs. Here Bex planted spring bulbs and roses, and can relax whenever she has a rare moment to herself. 'Before, we didn't have a space to just be in the garden. Now this is where I can come and sit, and I don't feel like I have to do anything.'

She confesses, though, that she has never been one to sit still for long, preferring to be doing something with her hands. Her latest experiments are in drying large whole flowers that typically don't dry well – such as physalis, pansies, cosmos and sweet peas – in sand. 'I went down a rabbit hole of finding the best sand, which is actually pet chinchilla bathing sand!'

Bex has also been investigating dyeing her own ribbons, as well as *hapa zome*, an ancient Japanese printing technique involving hammering flowers, petals and leaves on to fabric such as silk or linen. She recently took up pottery, and has previously dabbled in embroidery, knitting, sewing, painting and drawing. It will be interesting to see how her future endeavours unfold.

FACING TOP LEFT Dried flowers fill jars on every surface and hang from the ceiling in Bex's studio. **FACING TOP RIGHT** Bex's mood board behind her workbench with an array of vessels above. **FACING BOTTOM** Hellebores, fritillaries and other hard-to-dry flowers after Bex has preserved them perfectly using chinchilla bathing sand. **OVERLEAF** Bex must harvest flowers for drying after the flowers have opened, rather than in bud as for cut flowers.

A Little Book of Latin for Gardeners
Monty Don Gardening at Longmeadow

FARRAH STORR

'THOSE CHAIRS ARE never sat in,' says Farrah Storr, pointing to the stylish pair of green Fermob seats on her lawn. 'For me, enjoyment of the garden is not in the reflection – it's in the doing. I spend literally every single hour I can out here.'

The magazine editor turned tech sis hasn't been gardening for long, but what she lacks in experience, she more than makes up for in enthusiasm and commitment. 'I will garden from sunrise until the end of the day, when I can't move my fingers. For some people it might be enough to potter about with their bedding, but people like me go full garden mode; it becomes your life. There's a line I'm starting to cross from it being a hobby into an obsession. I go slightly to excess with things.'

This self-confessed propensity to perfectionism has led to Farrah winning many accolades, including the honour of an MBE, as well as writing a book and creating one of the biggest lifestyle newsletter-blogs in the world. Things Worth Knowing, which covers fashion, beauty, travel and personal essays, has tens of thousands of followers, and gives her just the sort of insights into user experience and market trends that she needs as Head of Substack International.

Originally from Manchester, she left home at eighteen to study French with English literature at King's College in London. 'My mother is English and my father was Pakistani, and he always wanted me to be a doctor or lawyer, or maybe an engineer, so although I wanted to be a writer, I was quiet about the arts.'

She did, however, have an inspiring example in her sister, Tasmina, who had trained in law but left to work in magazines. Suddenly, it seemed possible to make a living out of it. 'And university was instrumental in me getting down to London and doing all the sorts of free work experience you needed to get your foot in the door in those days.'

Her first job was at *Woman & Home*, and another role followed at *Good Housekeeping*. It was the golden era for women's glossies and also the heyday for lads' mags like *Loaded*, where Tasmina knew a young journalist called Will Storr. Her first attempt to matchmake the pair on a blind date was a total failure, but soon Farrah and Will became best friends and, eventually, much, much more.

They moved to Australia for four years, where Farrah worked on *New Woman* magazine. 'At that point, we thought we were going to have a family, and so we made a deal. We would go and see the world before we made the nest. It was hard to come back home, because Australia is all beauty and sunshine, but we thought it was time to start a family and out there really felt like the other end of the world.'

Will had started to find success as an author, and although Farrah was preparing to quit her career for motherhood, the opportunities kept appearing – first, launching a new title called *Women's Health* on short notice; then, turning around the celebrated but ailing *Cosmopolitan*. She smashed both. 'So, there was a fork in the road. I loved my job, but it took about 150 per cent of me. I didn't know if I wanted to be a mother enough to give it up.'

She became editor-in-chief of fashion bible *Elle UK* in 2019, not long before the pandemic changed the face of modern work. 'When we came out of Covid, I felt I needed to do something new.' A friend put her in touch with Hamish McKenzie, co-founder of Substack, who wanted someone to 'ignite the UK' for the paid-newsletter platform. Although the role wasn't very clear and was completely out of Farrah's

comfort zone ('I'm basically tech illiterate'), she took the risk. Having always been an advocate for making the media industry and the arts accessible to a broader range of people, she felt the platform's aim to promote culture and offer independence to talented writers was a mission worth supporting.

It involves a lot of travel, but she now mostly works remotely from her Kent home, a former servant's cottage in the grounds of what was once a large estate, with a garden of around a third of an acre. When she moved in, however, she barely noticed the outside space and was happy to let her two dogs, Jones and Parker, use it as they pleased. It was only when a friend retrained as a life coach and needed willing victims to practise on that the garden even got a look in.

'She did a pie chart of my life, and it was one big colour for work, with a tiny sliver for my husband. She said, "It's not going to be good for you if you just put everything into your job."' Farrah went home and looked out the window at her ravaged garden. 'I remember thinking that because my dad was a gardener, maybe I could garden. It appealed to me because I like flowers – they're beautiful, and I like aesthetic things. And that was it. I just went outside.'

It wasn't the most successful of starts. Convinced that every strappy leaf she could see was a weed, Farrah mistakenly pulled up all the flower bulbs. 'And then I wondered why, the next year, there was nothing in the garden. I was a nightmare.' With a little help from garden designer and writer Jo Arnell, however, things soon began to move in the right direction. 'Jo made me fall in love with the philosophy of gardening, and helped me understand the new dimension it could bring to my life. Bit by bit, I stopped buying handbags, and started spending my money on plants. Which has been ruinous.'

She fell in love with gardening's rhythms and constant forward motion, but also discovered what a balm it could be for her overactive mind. 'I go out there and instantly forget about everything else because I'm so absorbed in what's in front of me. It lifts me out of my head, which I spend an awful lot of time in. It's like a lifeline, and it becomes a need after a while.'

The garden is split into four areas around the house. The first thing you see on arrival is a tall brick wall – what remains of one of the biggest Victorian walled gardens in the UK – adorned with a vast 'niffed' specimen of *Rosa* 'Madame Alfred Carrière'.

FACING Fallen damsons decorate the brick path under the rustic wooden arch by Farrah's shed. **ABOVE** The tiny courtyard outside her greenhouse features several small raised beds for growing salads and other edibles, as well as pots of flowers for summer interest. **OVERLEAF** Farrah's summerhouse, the perfect place to read or write, lies at the end of a gravel path through the lawn and is attached to her little greenhouse. Lavender hummocks line the other path through the cutting garden.

In front of the house Farrah has created a shrub border for autumn, with acers and a fiery-foliaged liquidambar tree. 'It's what I look at out the kitchen window in the morning when I'm making a cup of tea, or when I drive in at night.'

Through the house is a many-windowed garden room with wood stove, where Farrah likes to write, and which looks out over a lawn framed with wavy-edged beds. These borders are packed with mixed planting including many clipped shrubs such as bay, lavender, box and pittosporum in green, dark red and variegated. It is her ode to a sort of Japanese-inspired garden, having been to Japan and seen its famous gardens and their meticulous attention to detail. 'They are the type of gardens I like and that made me feel calm. I'm not good with anything that's a bit wild or loose – it makes me feel really uncomfortable.'

It's no surprise, then, to discover that Farrah's soul garden is La Louve in Provence, created by retired Hermès designer Nicole de Vésian. 'It's had a massive influence on me. The garden has no flowers; it's all shapes. There's something about it that speaks to me. It's the most beautiful landscape I've ever seen in my life.'

'I go out there and instantly forget about everything else because I'm so absorbed in what's in front of me. It lifts me out of my head, which I spend an awful lot of time in.'

ABOVE A pretty French wirework-style table and chairs offer a place to rest in the cutting garden, which features beds of *Verbena bonariensis*, dahlias and sunflowers and is more relaxed in spirit than the more formal, ornamental section of the garden around the house. **FACING, CLOCKWISE FROM TOP LEFT** Farrah's greenhouse is dinky but offers enough space to sow seeds and pot on plants; one wall features her collection of cabbageware plates above the precious pelargonium of her father's that she kept going through cuttings; the main lawn is framed by wavy-edged beds containing many clipped structural shrubs and foliage plants; Farrah prefers moody, darker-toned flowers but made an exception for *Dahlia* 'Santa Claus'.

The ordered character of La Louve, all green clouds and pillows, is an obvious influence on Farrah's clipped balls and domes, but she does still have some blooms here, with annual tulips in spring followed by irises, roses and hydrangeas. 'I go for dark colours like burgundy or ruby, but nothing romantic or whimsical.'

The last area of the garden is found through a rust-coloured arch, where a series of productive raised beds feature flowers grown for cutting, such as sweet peas, zinnias and dahlias. Further down a brick path lined with hummocks of lavender lie Farrah's shed, summer house and a sweet little greenhouse, where she sows Beth's poppies and more on her potting bench, under a wall hung with cabbageware plates.

Although originally inspired to give gardening a go because of her father, her approach – ever active, always doing something – is quite different to his. 'He seemed at peace and very happy at the end of the day when he would stand in the kitchen and stare for hours at the garden. That's my abiding memory of him.'

When he died, this garden connection took on a deeper importance for Farrah. Consumed with grief, she started digging up plants from his garden. 'It was like a fever. I bought a trolley and put all these plants on the train with me from Manchester to Kent.' There was also a pelargonium he had looked after for years in a large stone pot, which her brother drove the length of the country to get to her – only to discover post-journey that it had detached from its roots. 'I was beside myself. I'd never grown cuttings before, but in a fit of desperation I decided to try and see if I could hold on to a piece of him.'

Thankfully, that precious cutting did take, and last year produced its first flower. As well as progressing her horticultural skills, it seems to have given more profound meaning to Farrah's gardening practice – though she still protests heartily that she is essentially just a control freak who does it for distraction and aesthetics – and prompted thoughts on the transient nature of placemaking.

'I'm making something here and it might not live on after I've gone, but maybe that's the beauty of it,' she says. 'There was a moment when I was the gardener, and whoever owns this house next, it will become their painting. There's sadness in that, but also, the older I get, the more I think there's something special about the idea that no one else will have the view that I do – this is how I see the world. Someone else will come along and they'll have a different vision. I'm at peace with that.'

ABOVE Farrah spends every moment she can gardening, as the pleasure for her is in the doing. **FACING** A large eucalyptus tree towers over the ornamental section of the garden, which feature a pond in the lawn and sculpted beds with box and pittosporum balls and acers, and flowers including white Japanese anemone 'Honorine Jobert' and dark-pink *Salvia* 'Love and Wishes'.

MATT COLLINS

'ALL MY HEROES come here,' says Matt Collins. As head gardener at the Garden Museum in London, he often meets the luminaries of the horticultural world when they visit for events. The museum, a deconsecrated church on the banks of the Thames, is a paean to the history and culture of gardening, with curated collections, everchanging exhibitions and an archive of interesting material. 'It's an amazing hub of gardeners, debate and conversation,' he says. 'A fascinating place that never stands still.'

What he doesn't love quite so much, perhaps, is the difficulties the location creates. 'It's a shade garden with quite challenging conditions, in that we're overhung by eight massive plane trees. It's super dry, and it gets covered in leaves on a daily basis. There's a particular spirit that you must have to garden here, because it's a bit mad that we would try to make a garden in what is effectively an urban woodland.'

The most exciting space is the courtyard garden, which was created in 2017 as part of the larger project to reimagine and extend the museum. 'It's a plant collector's garden of strange and curious plants, inspired by the Tradescants,' says Matt. The Tradescants were a father and son, both called John, who were essentially England's earliest garden celebrities – the Monty Dons of the seventeenth century.

In addition to being royal gardeners for Charles I, they travelled the world, from the Mediterranean and North Africa to the Arctic Circle and North America, botanizing and bringing back interesting plants. They were the first to introduce the tulip tree (*Liriodendron tulipifera*) and the red columbine (*Aquilegia canadensis*), among others.

As local residents, they were buried at St-Mary-at-Lambeth Church, beside Lambeth Palace, in an ornate tomb adorned with reminders of their travels, such as shells, a crocodile and some of the plants they introduced (though where and when they encountered the multiheaded hydra monster depicted on one side has never been answered).

In the 1970s, as the rundown church was in danger of being demolished, a keen Tradescant fan named Rosemary Nicholson came looking for their tomb, and decided to rescue the church and turn it into a museum dedicated to garden history. The churchyard was redesigned into a parterre garden by Lady Salisbury, including lots of seventeenth-century plants, with the concept that should the two plant hunters awaken from their eternal slumber, they would recognize everything around them.

The new courtyard, designed by Dan Pearson, also takes its lead from the Tradescants but has a different approach, reflecting on interesting plant introductions through the centuries, all the way up to the modern day with contemporary plant hunters such as Sue and Bleddyn Wynn-Jones of Crûg Farm and Nick Macer from Pan Global Plants. 'We wanted to impart the sensation of what it might have felt like to walk into the Tradescants' garden in the 1600s, and be surrounded by plants that are not familiar,' explains Matt.

The space, surrounded by glass, has its own microclimate that allows more tender plants to be grown. It is, essentially, a recreation of a Wardian case, the device plant hunters once used to bring specimens back home across the seas. There are yellow ginger lilies and bright red cannas, leafy schefflera, melianthus and tetrapanax, and a special tree dahlia, *D. tamaulipana*, that blooms in December with single pink flowers. In the underplanting, there are lots of delicate spring bulbs and ground-covering gems. Climbers including jasmine and passion flowers reach up the columns of the covered walkway, giving the feel of a contemporary cloister.

SACRED
TO THE MEMORY OF
WILLIAM BLIGH ESQUIRE F.R.S.
THE CELEBRATED NAVIGATOR
FROM OTAHEITE TO THE WEST INDIES
BRAVELY FOUGHT THE BATTLES OF HIS COUNTRY
AGED 64.

On the other side of the glass, by the cafe entrance, is another small woodland scheme with epimediums, hellebores and ipheions in spring and hydrangeas in summer; this gives way into the piazza garden designed by Christopher Bradley-Hole, with blocks of yew hedging and pockets of planting among the ledger stones.

By the street, facing the river, is Matt's own contribution: a dry garden. 'It's almost entirely things that I've seen growing in similar inhospitable environments, with Mediterranean and desert plants, and totally experimental.' Matt also looks after the community garden across the road, which is part of a wider project to green up the immediate area around the museum and work with the local council to engage with the community.

It all couldn't be more different than Matt's own garden at home in Hampshire. 'It's on chalk and completely exposed to the sun. The garden was an added extra, and I thought I wasn't going to do much with it. It was a backyard to put the kids into and let them make what they want of it. But I found that I couldn't leave it be. Other bits of the house have fallen apart, and most of life since having kids has radically shifted. It's a nuts period, but somehow there's been just about enough time to make the garden. And because it has such a different aspect to the one that we have here at the museum, it allows me to release this desire to grow certain plants.' It's in no way a designed garden, he says – just a couple of borders with lots of flowers – but it has almost all been grown from seed, cuttings or divisions.

While home, Matt loves to wander out into the surrounding countryside to experience a more raw, natural form of planting and collect seed. His wanderlust extends to many trips abroad to see plants in the wild, especially in North America, and these experiences are the fuel that power his other great passion: writing. As well as features and columns for various newspapers, magazines and journals, from the RHS magazine *The Garden* to *Wallpaper* and the *Guardian* newspaper, he has written two books about trees.

'My writing is quite personal, reflective and tied into natural history. I find writing goes hand in hand with gardening. When you are physically engaged or when you go for a walk, you tend to have the best ideas, and gardening fosters that imaginative and observational thought process.'

Matt was always interested in the arts, studying history of art at university, but his real passion was playing guitar in indie

PREVIOUS The courtyard garden in spring with pots of Meyer lemons and tulip 'Golden Artist', and a large, blooming *Melianthus major* by the tomb of Captain William Bligh. **FACING, CLOCKWISE FROM TOP LEFT** Dan Pearson's woodland scheme outside the cafe, under the huge plane trees; *Tetrapanax papyrifer* 'Rex'; one of three small greenhouses by the entrance; erigeron and libertia cope well with the dry, semi-shaded conditions amongst the churchyard tombs. **ABOVE** Matt designed this experimental area with dry garden planting.

'When you are physically engaged or when you go for a walk, you tend to have the best ideas.'

rock bands. Once he had graduated and found himself with no money, living back home with his parents in the doldrums of rural West Wales, that was all he could think about. 'I wanted to get a job, move to London and be in a band. I was hanging out with a friend who'd just got into gardening, and I realized maybe that's what I could do too – a physical job that could keep me outside and pay the bills.'

He decided to learn about making gardens and practised on his parents' blank canvas of a garden. They lived just down the road from the National Botanic Garden of Wales, so he went to study there. 'I got really obsessive about learning plants and botanical names, and really excited about it all. It got to the point where, although I made it back to London and was in bands for a bit, my drive slowly pivoted over to horticulture, and went up a notch.'

Initially, he worked in garden maintenance, doing the rounds in high-end north London gardens, before stumbling upon the Garden Museum. He asked about volunteering and discovered they were just about to launch their first traineeship. 'I applied, and got it, and spent a year here indulging all those interests. It was totally incredible.' After his traineeship, Matt moved on to manage a large private garden in Richmond designed by Mary Keen. 'I was the quintessential gardener in his quiet shed, completely on their own, and I was totally comfortable in that setting; but I also like having other gardeners to bounce ideas off and chat to about stuff.'

No surprise, then, that in 2014 he returned to the museum to become head gardener and run the trainee programme, and has been there ever since. The role is part-time, which suits Matt down to the ground, as it gives him time to dedicate to writing. 'It has introduced me to this whole other world of the more whimsical, fanciful nature of gardens – the theoretical garden that hangs separately from the physicality of it. The one that we write about and imagine, and dream about. The best bit is being immersed somewhere that's so dynamic. I love the pace of this place.'

ABOVE LEFT In Matt's own Hampshire garden he grows everything from hollyhocks and nepeta to *Lilium* 'Lady Alice'. **ABOVE RIGHT** Fennel and the almond tree *Prunus dulcis* 'Sultane' create height in the border than runs down the garden to Matt's propagation area by his shed. **FACING** Field scabious from seed gathered from a local meadow tangles with a curry plant while rose 'Madame Alfred Carrière' clothes the garden fence.

WILL TOMSON

YOU MAY THINK that you are worldly-wise – have travelled, done interesting jobs, been around a bit – but then you meet Will Tomson and realize you haven't really lived. 'I have had a lot of random jobs,' he confirms, and hints at stints on a whale-watching boat and as a songwriting teacher. He has worked as a dog-sledding guide in Canada, learned bonsai from a master in Japan and dived for sea slugs in Mozambique, as well as grafting in various places as a labourer. It's been a long and winding road to his true calling as a landscape designer.

Now based back where he grew up, near Sheffield in South Yorkshire, he has finally stopped moving and focused on creating his own personal haven at Berrywell, a cloistered secret garden around an old railwayman's shack. Here he has built a new larch-clad cabin, which he rents out for self-catering, and an astonishing small natural swimming pond as the centrepiece of a beautiful wild garden.

His restless job-hopping was not, as might be assumed, a symptom of low academic achievement, but quite the opposite – Will is one of those quietly super-intelligent people who aced his A levels and had his pick of any course, including medicine. He chose biochemistry ('It was the next hardest thing'), and because of his grades was able to take his first year off to backpack around New Zealand.

'So I went straight into second year biochemistry, and it was horrible. I hated it so much I dropped out.' He did not receive a hero's welcome back home, where his family and friends, in the best possible way, started putting pressure on him. 'They were like, "What are you doing? You're wasting your time working in a tissue factory."' He was staying with his best friend Jono, whose father pulled out a prospectus and pushed Will to go back and study something that would further his interest in nature, like ecology. Will realized he was right, and scrambled to get back on track. 'I had to grovel to Edinburgh University to let me back in, but they did.'

After his degree, there was more travelling and a segue into youth and community work on city farms, for arts organizations and social enterprises. It resulted in Will doing things he could never have foreseen, such as creating a show garden and leading a group of at-risk teens on a landscape project in Ayrshire. 'It was rewarding work seeing these young people transform.'

That role turned into several years leading an urban greening project in Glasgow, while also pursuing his other great love of music. 'I didn't start playing guitar until I was seventeen but as a child I played in brass bands. I used to hate it, but I'm so grateful for it now, because it taught me how to read music.'

Part of the same Sheffield cohort that produced indie sleaze legends Arctic Monkeys, he always loved jamming with his friends and writing songs. He even taught music-making as part of his youth work, but never performed until one evening when he walked into an open mic night, signed up and played his first song in front of people. 'That got me over the fear, and I started playing gigs and festivals in a band.'

Music may be an essential creative outlet for Will, but it was never the primary bill-payer of his portfolio career, and as time went on his passion for plants and gardens began to take over. He really wanted to get better at garden design and improve his knowledge, and a friend recommended the horticulture and plantsmanship course at the Royal Botanic Garden Edinburgh. He studied while he worked, doing it part time over three years, and was delighted to find that he actually enjoyed academic life for the first time. 'I was a total nerd, absolutely absorbing it all.'

At the same time, he got an allotment to experiment with planting, and bothered landscapers for advice and work so he could fill in his gaps in construction skills. He credits Dug MacLeod from Stone Wood Water Light and designer Tracy McQue as exceptionally generous mentors who gave him support and encouragement, showed him what it meant to be professional and how to manage projects.

Another game-changer for Will was his acceptance on the Triad Fellowship, which saw him spend a year in American, Japanese and UK heritage gardens. Japan was particularly influential, filled with eye-opening experiences like working with the oldest garden maintenance company in Kyoto on the famous temple gardens, at a prestigious ikebana school and with a bonsai specialist in the mountains.

'I learned so much about the deep culture of Japan and all the things that go into a garden. The concepts I learned over there completely changed the way I think about design. It's the difference between appreciating the detailed beauty of an individual plant versus the British way of using a mass effect.' At Berrywell he has added a tiny dry garden, with ripples raked into gravel around a mossy stone, in homage to these Japanese gardens he so loved.

On returning from the fellowship, he volunteered on the build of designer Chris Beardshaw's show garden at the Chelsea Flower Show, and that led to a job in Chris's design studio in the Cotswolds. But a yearning to settle down was starting to build in Will. On one trip home to Sheffield, he idly wondered what the local house prices were like. 'Searching online, this place was the first thing that came up, and the cheapest, and it turned out that it was going to auction at the end of that week. It was just around the corner from my mum's, but I had never seen it before. The only viewing, it said, was Wednesday at 2 pm, and I was reading this at ten minutes to two on Wednesday. So I closed my laptop and walked down the track.'

Straight away he could tell the rundown old house with its overgrown plot was his dream. 'There were no neighbours, and it had water, electricity and established trees making a beautiful frame around it.' Unfortunately, there were lots of other people looking at it too, and many red flags. The deeds had been lost, so no one knew who owned the bordering land with access to the road. 'In the end that was a godsend, because it made it unsuitable for all the developers who were looking at it.'

Will wanted to buy it more than anything, but there was one major problem – he simply didn't have the money. He pooled his meagre savings, went to anyone he could borrow from and got a loan from his close friend James, managing to pull together the promise of £80,000 in time for the auction. 'It was the most stressful thing I have ever experienced in my life. Someone else was bidding against me, and it went up and up. They tapped out at £75,000, and my first thought was, "Oh my god, what have I done? That's all my money, and I can't even live in it yet as it's not suitable for habitation."'

It was late 2019 and Covid was on the horizon. Will moved in with his sister just in time for lockdown, and spent his days fixing up his tumble-down new house and making the garden. When he arrived, there was a sea of waist-high grass littered with old electrical goods – 'You'd swear they had never been to the tip' – with the dominant feature a row of hulking Leylandii trees.

'I could see there was a beautiful black walnut tree underneath as well as a hawthorn and a yew. All these trees were being smothered, so the first thing was to get the Leylandii down. That changed the feel of the garden. It let in more light and gave space to those trees. And as soon as I did that, I knew that I was going to put another building there.'

Will designed his new cabin to wrap gently around the existing walnut tree, with all the windows looking out on to the garden and a deck out front for sitting on. 'I wanted it to feel like you're really in the garden, with a seamless boundary between the indoors and out.' The plan was to hire it out to make enough to rebuild the old house, and the cabin has proved one of the most loved properties on Airbnb. After all, who wouldn't want a dip in a private swimming pond on their mini break?

Typically more lake than pond sized, and beyond the means of most DIYers, these natural pools use plants as biological filters instead of chemicals, keeping them clear and healthy for swimming while boosting biodiversity. 'I knew I wanted a big body of water that would become the heart of the garden, reflecting the sky and bringing in wildlife,' says Will. To figure out how to make his own, he read books and went on a course

ABOVE Will built the cabin around an existing black walnut tree. A large yew bush and a hawthorn tree grow either side.

'I really like when you let nature make the decision of where things should go. To me, that's the interesting part of gardening.'

PREVIOUS The DIY swimming pond is framed by borders of robust perennials including blue *Aconitum* and white *Leucanthemum* daisies. **FACING, CLOCKWISE FROM TOP LEFT** A Japanese dry garden (*karesansui*) by Will's sauna, modelled on the smallest dry garden in Japan, Totekiko; green groundcovers mind-your-own-business and *Selaginella helvetica*; native plants such as wild carrot are encouraged to grow and seed through the cultivated garden plants, like daylilies. **ABOVE** An old railway sleeper set upright on the winter solstice so that the sunrise can be observed through the hole. It sits by a small shallow pond that provides an additional wet habitat, surrounded by moisture-loving plants such as *Rheum palmatum* and *Darmera peltata*.

with David Pagan Butler – known for inventing a low-cost, low-energy, bubble-circulation system and showing thousands of people how to make their own pool on his YouTube channel.

Will was getting a digger in to sort out his septic tank and took the opportunity to dig out the 8 × 5 metre (26 × 16 foot) space for the pond at the same time, tipping the spoil straight on to a problem patch of ground elder. It was a laborious, time-consuming feat for him and his helpers to finesse the design with spades, and having to painstakingly wash tons of gravel by hand for the regeneration zone, but it was all worth it in the end.

Now Will and his guests can be at one with nature, swimming or just gently floating in the water surrounded by glorious meadow-like planting. 'My plants aren't anything out of the ordinary, but they work together to give that naturalistic feel. My style now is letting a lot of native plants that might be seen as weeds grow and go through everything else, so I use robust perennials that are going to be able to deal with that, like ox-eye daisies and echinops. It's pretty low maintenance.'

One striking inclusion is yellow-flowered common ragwort, considered a field weed with a bad reputation for being toxic to horses and livestock. In a garden setting, however, it can be a wonderful wild flower and valuable forage for cinnabar moth caterpillars. Will also allows some rosebay willowherb as food for the caterpillars of elephant hawk moths. 'I really like when you let nature make the decision of where things should go. To me, that's the interesting part of gardening. It doesn't want to be static – it wants to change.'

Although Will has since set up his own design-and-build practice creating gardens for people all over the country, this special plot – his first real garden – continues to hold him in its thrall. 'I'm obsessive about this space. That desire to create is what I find fun, and I really enjoy gardening. I love having my hands in the soil and working outside. And a garden is never finished, is it? It's like when you're writing a bit of music: you've got the main structure, but then once you start writing the lyrics, you might have to go back and change the tune. That's the process of design, and I don't like to put a full stop on it.'

ABOVE Cinnabar moth caterpillars happily gorging on ragwort. **FACING** The spent seedheads of foxgloves reach up from the planting around the pond, which includes pink *Campanula lactiflora* 'Loddon Anna', yellow golden rod and calamagrostis grass. **OVERLEAF** The boardwalk cuts through the dry swales near the pond at Birch Farm, where Josh Sparkes is building habitats with diverse topographies.

INDEX

INDEX

ACKNOWLEDGMENTS

The author and photographer would like to express our humble thanks to the gardeners and growers who graciously welcomed us into their plots, homes, studios and lives in the making of this book. It has been a deeply personal project for all of us and we are grateful for their trust, honesty and openness in sharing not just their gardens but also their stories. We would also like to thank the extended team members and owners at some of the open and public gardens such as the Horniman Museum, Knepp, the Garden Museum and The Hepworth Wakefield for facilitating our visits. Special thanks go to our fantastic team at Frances Lincoln – Alice Graham, Michael Brunström and Isabel Eeles – who have exhibited boundless patience and excellent judgement in all matters. Thank you, too, to our parents, siblings, friends and colleagues for their support and words of encouragement along the way. And finally, we'd like to dedicate this book to our wonderful daughter Eirlys, our little gardener, who we hope will be inspired to continue to find ways to explore her own creativity – because we believe that is a superpower and the secret to a fulfilling life.

Quarto

First published in 2026 by Frances Lincoln,
an imprint of The Quarto Group.
One Triptych Place, London, SE1 9SH,
United Kingdom
T (0)20 7700 9000
www.Quarto.com
EEA Representation, WTS Tax d.o.o., Žanova ulica 3, 4000 Kranj, Slovenia
www.wts-tax.si

A catalogue record for this book is available from the British Library.

ISBN 978-1-83600-404-2
Ebook ISBN 978-1-83600-405-9

10 9 8 7 6 5 4 3 2 1

Design: DSGN DEPT.
Publisher: Philip Cooper
Editorial Director: Alice Graham
Senior Editor: Michael Brunström
Senior Designer: Isabel Eeles
Senior Production Controller: Rohana Yusof

Printed in Guangdong, China TT062026

FSC www.fsc.org MIX Paper | Supporting responsible forestry FSC® C016973

STEPHANIE MAHON is Editor of *Gardens Illustrated* magazine and host of the *Talking Gardens* podcast. She has won many accolades including both BSME Editor of the Year and Garden Media Guild Journalist of the Year twice, and is author of four other books including *Wild Gardens: Inspired by Nature*, as well as editor of the *Gardens Illustrated* book *The New Beautiful*. Previously editor of *The English Garden* magazine and the *Garden Design Journal*, Stephanie has also written for newspapers such as *The Telegraph*, *The Sunday Times* and *The Guardian* and many national magazines. She does try to do things not related to plants and gardens in her spare time, but usually fails miserably.

JOHN CAMPBELL is an award-winning photographer and filmmaker who now specializes in gardens, having fallen in love with documenting the work of their creators and curators. His images have been exhibited on the vast displays in Times Square, New York, and published in magazines including *Country Life*, *Country Homes & Gardens*, *The English Garden* and *Gardens Illustrated*. John's previous books include *Buckingham Palace: A Royal Garden* – the first official book, photographing the famous royal London garden and its gardeners throughout the seasons – and his film work includes feature-length documentaries for *Garden Masterclass*.